Social Entrepreneurship

Social Entrepreneurship

A Sustainable Christian Mission Tool

Manoj Parajuli

Christian World Imprints

First Published in 2020 by

Christian World Imprints
Christian Publishing & Books from India
C-3, Wazirpur Industrial Area
Delhi-110052
cwidelhi2017@gmail.com
info@christianworldimprints.com
www.ChristianWorldImprints.com
Phone: +91 11 41526079

ISBN: 978-93-5148-476-9

Printed in India.

Contents

Introduction

Uttrakhand is the 27th state of India, known as '*Dev Bhoomi*' which means the "land of gods." Christianity had reached this land in 1624, but became more prominent in the 1814. Despite this, impact of Christianity has been very slow and the presence of Christians in these mountains is less. Missions work has been done through various kinds of social work, education, and medical avenues, but there has not been much impact.

I have been a missionary in Uttrakhand for the past eighteen years. I was 16 years old when I came here and started working along with "Community of Nation, Church." I have seen and experienced mission work ups and downs, based on funding coming from the west. However, we often talk about self-sustaining, self-governing and self-propagating mission work not only in India but throughout the world; in reality, many times, mission works are very much dependent on donors.

Workers, who are on a mission field and visit house after house or village after village, to share the Gospel, are often seen Struggling with financial hardship. This is particularly true among native missionaries. They do not have proper financial resources, but instead they are very much dependent on some kind of mission organization's support which helps them to barely survive. They are seen as people who do not have financial income source but somehow they survive and propagate Christianity.

This kind of situation invites unnecessary attention and trouble upon workers from anti-Christian government or the people group within their own community from another faith.

Due to organizational structure and its administrative cost, lots of resources are used in organizing it rather than using the resources for the very mission work. Not only that, people who are holding the higher post enjoy the resources but those who are at the lower end including the indigenous workers who are actually putting blood, sweat, and tears into the mission field to reach out to the unreached people group, survive on little resources.

Many missionaries are now trying to use the BUSINESS model for mission. However, it is a personal conviction or call if someone does business for the cause of mission. For example, if someone wants to become a doctor and open a hospital or clinic for the cause of mission. These are wonderful things where all Christians are obligated to do so, whatever profession they are in. Social entrepreneurship is based on the concept of making wealth within the community for the community, which will not abuse the environment, rather it goes towards sustainability. It brings order in a chaotic situation. Christian Social Entrepreneurship is very much Missional in its nature. This can be the best tool for modern mission.

Social entrepreneurship combats social issues by the application of business methods to achieve financial sustainability while seeking to create a social impact. For Christian missionaries, this blending of a business model can be a valuable tool to help sustain an organization while at the same time bearing witness in particular places as missionaries. The overall purpose of this book is to introduce Social Entrepreneurship as a sustainable tool, which is both Missional and Biblical in terms of its nature. The concluding remarks of this book "Developing Social Entrepreneurship as a Tool for an Innovative and Sustainable Christian Mission Work" has been brought out throughout this book. As you go through the book, it will help you understand Christian social entrepreneurship through theoretical, Missional, biblical, theological perspective.

"Social entrepreneurs might just prove to be the missing missionaries that we need for a fair and just society."

– Dr. R.K. Pachauri

Chapter 1

Theoretical Consideration of Social Entrepreneurship

The determination and task of a missionary is a holistic presentation of the gospel. Gospel is an all-inclusive concern for the welfare of mankind that includes three imperatives - *body, soul,* and *spirit.* The reason for stating this is based on the fact that God has concern not only for our spiritual emancipation but also socio-political and economic emancipation. Another reason for this can be that we are inevitably and constantly interacting within a society.

Especially in our time of technological innovation and rapid globalization, it is important to re-evaluate our mission approach. This re-evaluation will be a consideration of mission undertaking in the past and that of mission in a globalized world. In a globalized world, we have become more intertwined with others, and perhaps our lives are defined through our interaction with religious, social and governmental institutions such as schools, hospitals, rehabilitation and counselling centers, orphanages, colleges, churches, community service groups and NGOs, banks, etc. This new shape of our world has helped us deliberate the need for a social oriented mission.

Having said this, it is also important at this juncture to address the issue of social disparity. Particularly in India, many people are victims to this contrasted status of social existence. It is rational to say that globalization has improved and has connected societies, but it has also adversely affected the lives of those in the rural areas and the backward classes of society. There are several villages where stable economy or sustainable economy is still out of reach. Life is basically defined by hard labor, low income, illiteracy, and absence of vocational and industrial/agricultural skills. Therefore, with an intent to escape from these hardships, many people migrate to the cities. As a result, cities of India are swarming with slums. There are numerous people below poverty line; illiteracy, unemployment, corruption, and underdevelopment, are all rampant and increasing. Introduction of indigenous enterprises becomes the need of the hour. This is a Macedonian call for entrepreneurs, but a risk where only few would be bold enough to take UP this venture. The need of the people combined with the reluctance of government (agencies, enterprises, entrepreneurs) widened the gap between the rich and the poor. The economic pressure is killing the poor and is exacerbated each passing minute.

It is within this context that mission work is placed. Besides social hardships, there are additional factors at play such as, natural disasters, epidemic disease/sickness, wars and conflicts etc. In relation to these challenges, mission work and agencies mostly and merely serve as intermediaries or agents that address the social needs of the poor and needy based on the resources that were pooled together by generous donors. Such a work of charity is commendable, but on the other hand, not sustainable. For instance, when the funding stops the works cease to proceed. The need for a sustainable mission work that address the social needs of the people becomes a coveted mission tool. There is also a requirement of those social entrepreneurs who would set aside their personal greed and stand on behalf of the poor, downtrodden, and oppressed section of the society. Social entrepreneurship is, I believe, a handy tool for sustaining mission work in such a context as well as a beacon of hope for the neglected and underprivileged section of the society.

1.1. Entrepreneur/Entrepreneurship

Entrepreneurship is concerned with the examination of how, by whom, and with what effects opportunities can engender future goods and accommodations to be discovered, evaluated, and exploited. Kevin D. Johnson in "*The Entrepreneur Mind...*" states that entrepreneurs are job makers not job seekers, and they boldly take risk and define the market, but do not follow the market. According to Jean Baptiste, a French Economist, they became a force that sustains and promote a higher productivity and greater yield. Furthermore, Oxford English dictionary defines an entrepreneur as "a person who attempts to profit by risk and initiative."

According to Peter Drucker, a well-known economist, "an entrepreneur is someone who sees and uses opportunities given... always searches for change, responds to it, and exploits it as an opportunity." An entrepreneur sought for opportunities detached from administrative managers and their own initial resources. According to Hans Jobst Pleitner, this process involves; the use of opportunities, taking risks, coordination of resources, generation of jobs, development and exploitation of innovations, and value creation.

Management in entrepreneurship is motivated by the implementation of imaginative creativity. The management perceives an opportunity for a new product, then organizes and assumes the financial risks. It is not essential to have a formal training for becoming an entrepreneur, but it is indispensable to look beyond to the place where opportunities are created, and creating something out of nothing. On the success of an entrepreneur, Rosabeth Moss Kanter, a management Guru and Professor at Harvard Business School, developed four F's to define entrepreneurial success. They are:

a) *Founders*-every startup company must have a first class team of entrepreneurs who have the same goal and direction
b) *Focused*-they are focused on what their client needs the most
c) *Fast*-they launch the venture after good research, and take quick decisions in times of need
d) *Flexible*-they keep an open-minded for any change

These four F's were further developed by William D. Bygrave, who states that entrepreneurs are *forever-innovating,* they keep thinking since they are tireless innovators; *flat,* all members work hard for the venture; *frugal,* they keep costs down; *friendly* because they want to please their customers; and they are *fun* because they work together for the cause of giving birth to their dreams. In the process of becoming a successful entrepreneurs, these principles of F's will prove to be of great help.

1.2. Social Entrepreneur

A famous line by Victor Hugo reads "There is one thing stronger than all the armies in the world, and that is an idea whose time has to come." Such an idea is born out of an individual who, as often stated, has the stubbornness to challenge the old system and persuade others of his/her idea for change. Entrepreneurs are revolutionary people who have the ability and agility to spread their ideas and touch the society, move hearts, shift perceptions and inspire people.

Social entrepreneurs are revolutionaries with unique ability to perceive opportunities and solutions to complex and perpetual social issues. As entrepreneurs with social mission, theirs can be called as 'mainstream approach.' Dees defines an 'idealized' version of social entrepreneurs as "change agents in the social sector by adopting a mission to create and sustain social value, not just private value, recognizing and relentlessly pursuing new opportunities to serve that mission engaging in a process of continuous innovation, adaptation, and learning, acting boldly without being limited by resources currently in hand and exhibiting a heightened sense of accountability to the constituencies served and for the outcomes created".

'Mainstream approach' entrepreneurship develops a sense of accountability to their mission and shareholders. They count it as their task to address and develop social injustices such as poverty, social ills, and thus renovation of the environment. Social entrepreneurship in this sense is reasonably a concern for the welfare of others. It is not a means of self-promotion or self-interest gains, and hence profit becomes a peripheral motive.

There are three types of social entrepreneurs according to scholars: a) Social Bricoleur, b) Social Constructionist, and c) Social

Engineer. This classification is based on their approach to a given opportunity, even though they all have a common goal to impact the society with their agenda and the resources available.

1. *Social Bricoleurs* typically focus on discovering and addressing local needs through an awareness of both local environmental conditions and local resources.
2. *Social Constructionists* are acting in a more institutionalized perspective by addressing gaps in the provision of socially significant products. They introduce innovations leading to the renewal of large scale social systems. Their advantage does not come from local knowledge, like in the case of Social Bricoleurs, but from the way these entrepreneurs recognize opportunities to address the social issues, often by creating and influencing different processes.
3. *Social Engineers* embrace innovation that will be disruptive in order to create social equilibrium. They recognize and address large scale systemic problems within existing social structures. Social Engineers differ from the other two types of social entrepreneurs because they have a revolutionary impact on the social systems and structures.

1.2.1. Characteristics and Capacity of Social Entrepreneurs

Social entrepreneurs are characteristically motivated by the plight of a society. They consider themselves obligated to create a desirable and rightful enterprise that addresses and identifies social problems. This sense of 'perceived desirability' became a launching pad for their venture towards building a stable society through social enterprises. Following are some of the characteristics of social entrepreneurship:

Social Vision: A sense of responsibility and emotional connection of fighting for a social or environmental cause considered just. This requires considerable engagement, prompting people to see long term opportunities and to spare no expense in achieving lasting change. Social vision is what guides social entrepreneurs, and keep other motivations away that could distract them from the social aim of the entrepreneur's initiative.

Sustainable Practices: This dimension is borne of awareness that people and organizations are interconnected and form a part of a single ecosystem. Everything is related and the action of one affects others in some way. This focus seeks to find a balance between economic, social, and environmental interests. This entails constant dedication to seeking solutions that achieve the result through responsible innovation. Environmental concern is fundamental in this dimension. Social entrepreneurs take time to fix the problem with the intention of sustainable, profitable, renewal, and long lasting improvements.

Ability to Develop Social Networks: Social support or social networks refer to positive formal or informal relationships with people in one's environment, and the potential of what can be achieved with their support. Active participation in social networks enables collective learning which can furnish the entrepreneur with valuable knowledge, advice and information towards effective solutions. Positive interpersonal relations are also conducive to gaining the trust and respect of many people. A good reputation is a key for the social entrepreneur as this can translate into future network connections, for e.g., future investors.

Innovation Capacity: Due to limited resources, social entrepreneurs are often driven by a strong urge to generate positive changes for the society by seeking innovative solutions to accomplish their goals. Moreover, their social aim breaks the traditional mold of pursuing economic objectives which naturally leads to empowerment for alternative innovation. To this end, for example, many social entrepreneurs seek to address the needs of underserved markets, such as "the bottom of the pyramid". As a result, they must find new ways to reach these by reconsidering different aspects of the business model, distribution channels, the product or service, forms of payment, etc. Social entrepreneurs look for innovative ways to ensure that their ventures create social value and obtain needed resources and funding as long as they are creating value. They do not find satisfaction in creating only one thing or settling into one way of doing things; they are constantly reevaluating and innovating new products to make a difference and find that zeal that comes from taking new risks. Social Entrepreneurs find or create opportunity.

Where there is chaos and need, there you find crisis and opportunity both. Social Entrepreneurs take hold of the opportunity to bring order, peace, and harmony to make this earth "a better place to live".

They Take Risks to Start New Ventures: Social entrepreneurs are often driven by the needs around them; they move ahead with all the resources they have in their hands by taking risk. They are open for the financial charity as well as exploitation of marketing since they are not controlled by any means and custom.

Ability to Generate Financial Returns: Finally, the capacity to generate financial returns is basic for the social entrepreneur as this guarantees organization's sustainability. The social aim will always be foremost; nonetheless, the financial aspect is a necessary part of achieving this aim, and for covering a greater proportion of the population. Social entrepreneurs take steps to ensure that they are creating value. They seek to provide real social improvements to their beneficiaries and their communities, as well as an attractive social and/or financial return to their investors. And, although they may act locally, their actions have a very real potential to stimulate global improvements in their chosen arena.

1.2.2. Qualities of Successful Social Entrepreneurs

The success of an entrepreneur is measures by a determination to achieve a long term goal. Following are qualities that describe a successful entrepreneur:

a) Willingness to Self-Correct

Because of their motivation, highly successful entrepreneurs are highly self-correcting. It takes a combination of hard-headedness, humility, and courage to stop and say, "This isn't working" or "Our assumptions were wrong," particularly when the funding is linked to accomplishing pre-existing plans. However, when problems occur, social entrepreneurs want to know primarily what happened and what needs to be fixed rather than focusing on who to blame for the problem.

b) Willingness to Cross Disciplinary Boundaries

Independence from established structures not only helps social entrepreneurs escape limitations, it also gives them the freedom to combine resources in new ways. Indeed, one of the primary functions of social entrepreneurs is to serve as a sort of social alchemist, to create new social compounds. When social entrepreneurs face new challenges, they cross the old boundaries bringing all kinds of expertise from different spheres with different experiences to create solutions.

c) Willingness to Work Quietly

Many social entrepreneurs spend decades steadily advancing their ideas, influencing people in small groups or one to one, therefore their work is often difficult to understand and measuring its impact is a difficult. Often they are recognized only after years working under the radar. Their work becomes more powerful when they inspire others to join their own ideas to bring social change. "The beauty of demonstrating positive pathways is that it is possible to redirect human energy without telling people what to do."

d) Willingness to Share Credit

For entrepreneurs, willingness to share credit is imperative to success because the more credit they share, the more people typically would want to help them. If the entrepreneur's true intention is simply to make a change happen, then sharing credit will come naturally. However, if the true intention is to be recognized as having been *the* person to make change happen, than sharing credit may run against the grain.

1.3. Social Entrepreneurship

Social essential is perceptible by two essential factors - *social goals* and *social change.* Social entrepreneurship is an undertaking without a prior intent of profit. With an innovative and determinative approach, it is a combination of social mission and business management. It aims at creating social values and breaking down of existing social patterns. Based on existing research in social organizational management, economics, and strategic management, Scott Helm (2007) developed the idea that social entrepreneurship could be built within the social sector. He states that social entrepreneurship is the driving force of non-profit organizations that engenders value and change in the social sector, community, or industry through the combination of innovation and risk-taking attitude. Most importantly, social entrepreneurship is a blend of ideologies and practices between social and economic value. It is driven with the task to generate sustainable resources to support mission by engaging market forces to work for the nonprofit sector, allowing for greater flexibility by bringing in unrestricted revenue, decreasing dependence on the external funding community, and devising new ways to manipulate existing assets. The scope of social entrepreneurship is very broad. Leading social entrepreneurs today have attempted to define specific characteristics of three different types of this work. We can categorize them as profit, nonprofit and hybrid models.

a) *Profit:* Working within the private sector gives social entrepreneurs an advantage in terms of the direction they take in planning, profit, and innovation. Private social entrepreneurs do not necessarily set up purely social enterprises, but they integrate social values into their businesses. They must also wrestle with the dilemma of trying to run a business that is attempting to make a profit, and a business that is pursuing a social mission at the same time. However, there are several legal structures available to entrepreneurs who can choose to structure their venture as a profit such as 'Habitat for Humanity', and others like them. These kind of ventures achieve their primary social or environmental mission using business methods. Two primary characteristics distinguish these organizations: a commitment to social purpose and a reliance on earned income for the benefit of society.

b) *Not-for-profit:* Despite their name, nonprofit organizations are not excluded from generating a profit. They can produce excess revenue as long as they observe the "private inurement doctrine." This legal restriction holds that a nonprofit cannot distribute its earning amongst its investors and owners. These earnings must be poured back into the organization in pursuit of its mission. This is the chief distinction between a nonprofit and a for profit organization. According to Lead Beater, the not-for-profit sector is the most fertile source for social entrepreneurship, and in fact, social entrepreneurships have been going on in the sector for a long time.

c) *Hybrids:* As the name implies, hybrid structures assumed by social ventures represent various combinations of structural elements from nonprofit, for-profit, and/or government organizations. These hybrids are innovative structures of social mission that can offer effective solutions. The social entrepreneurs who create these structures generally seek greater legal and financial flexibility for pursuing their missions. New hybrid structures are being developed and tested on a regular basis and are limited only by imagination and the law.

1.3.1. Social Entrepreneurship and Business Entrepreneurship

Social entrepreneurship is a social oriented undertaking with a purpose to transform the society. This vision influences how they measure prosperity and how they structure their enterprise. This made them distinctive from a business entrepreneurship. Unlike a business oriented entrepreneur they do not receive the same kind of market feedback. As in the case of business entrepreneurship, there is a production of efficient value for the customer which ultimately replaces the investors in the a form of profit, but social enterprises reinvest that benefit for the profit of the society. For this reason, in social entrepreneurship, profit is not a standard for organizational performance, rather success is measured based on the extent to which they create social value. They are actors of social change.

1.3.2. Characteristics of Social Entrepreneurship

Social entrepreneurship understands that environmental and social solutions have irregular limited period of effectiveness. In this case, there is a necessity for competition in market ecosystems particularly when there are less resources. Social entrepreneurs take social inventions or their creativity, whether they are the creators or not, and implement them as a means to problem solving and transformative change. Despite the fact that a social innovation must have a market, the chief test of its value lies in its potential to solve a social or environmental problem. Social Entrepreneurs are always in search of social excellence for example, *Ashoka Foundation* has been supporting around 200 social entrepreneurs in India, Indonesia, and Brazil and many other countries to solve social problems.

Some of the creative solutions provided by social entrepreneurship are - *putting children in charge.* This strategy creates enthusiasm among the youth and develops skills and confidence. Through *enlisting 'barefoot' professionals,* entrepreneurs can devise cost-effective ways to deliver basic services. Having no working skills in themselves, these barefoot professionals collaborate with social entrepreneurs and are benefitted by it. This strategy is a redirection of the creative energies of people within communities. There is also a *designing of new legal framework for environmental reform.* This process, for instance, helps the farmers to cease the use of unhealthy fertilizers and antibiotics in farming, and retains the natural and organic forms of healthy farm practices. Social entrepreneurship also *helps small producers capture greater profits.* Not all population of the poor section are engaged in industrial works, but also in small scale trade and self-employment. The intent of social entrepreneurship is to alleviate poverty among such groups and help them benefit and increase products in their trade and commerce. Some, like Muhammad Yunus, of Grameen Bank, focus on access to capital. With small amounts of capital, villagers can purchase assets, increase their productive capacity, and gain profits that historically have accrued to money lenders and landowners.

Finally, social entrepreneurship is sought for *linking citizens, government, and business sector for comprehensive solutions.* Social entrepreneurs often create tremendous value when they meet very basic humanitarian needs; for example, providing medicines or food can be a matter of life or death for those who receive them. Another example is AIDS vaccines which are given through the International

AIDS Vaccine Initiative. Both the government and local citizens are partnering together is this initiative to see lives changed and communities benefited. It is a cooperative approach.

1.3.3. Social Entrepreneurship Process Model Theory

Process model, among many others, is an attempt to make that which is complex more manageable. Process Model Theory takes place in two stages:

Stage One: Idea (Need, Capacity, and Motivation)

An entrepreneur in this stage is moved with a desire to do something for the needy community. His desire is followed by a decision to venture, pooling all his resources, and with a motivation to achieve his purpose of addressing and meeting the needs of people. Although this new venture involves risks, there are human resources, local resources, market, and capital investment to benefit him in his perceived opportunity to achieve social mission.

Stage Two: Mission (Opportunity, People, Resources)

Social entrepreneurs see an opportunity in social crisis despite the perilous bearings pertaining to it. Yet, he ventures out into this crisis motivated by opportunity and the desire for providing a sustainable solution by employing local resources. They study the market, local resources, and workforce to meet his end. In social entrepreneurship all variables such as politics, culture, economic environment, social norms, and legal monetary systems are blended together into a single form to achieve the goals. This model which we have labeled the Social Entrepreneurship Process Model will be used to guide our thinking. Social entrepreneurs use the pursuit of economic value as a tool for achieving their social mission and for creating and sustaining social value.

Conclusion

Social entrepreneurship is a vital tool for mission especially since charity works are not sustainable and fulfilling. Charity works operate under a limited time period and are solely dependent on the assistance of others. Social entrepreneurship ensures the opposite. It is an instrument that focuses on society - the poor and the helpless therein, thereby finding solutions that would eventually enable a person to self-support and sustain himself.

While the existing charity oriented socio-mission addresses and provides a temporal solution to social struggles, social entrepreneurship will tend to be an enduring solution. Charity in mission work produces a dependent group of people which often ends with frustration and disappointment when an organization or charitable trust could no longer answer their problems. It is far more a greater mission work to create an independent, strong, and healthy community; better to educate on how to generate resources than to constraint a community of their growth with our charities, and gave them false hope with our temporal solutions to their enduring problems.

Now, after our discussion on entrepreneurship, and particularly social entrepreneurship, it would be fitting here to state that a redefinition of our mission strategy with this as a tool would enable us to produce a sustainable and effective work. In societies where people struggle for their lives, we can no longer turn blind to their plight but must help them with finding a solution (a way out). This aspect is very much part and parcel of God's heartbeat, '*mission.*'

In line with our discussion on the characteristics, methods, qualities of entrepreneurship, we can count ourselves to be more than capable of venturing into an uncharted territory, taking all the risks, pouring all our resources, but only to the Glory of God, the extension of His Kingdom, and the improvement of society of men.

Chapter 2

Missional Basis for Social Entrepreneurship

It is true when our Lord Jesus said that 'the poor will always be with us.' For many centuries, government and various organizations have been fighting this weapon of mass destruction called *poverty.* Concentration, when it comes to economic development is basically at the forefront of life-expectancy, education, and health standards. In this scenario, social entrepreneurship became a new field of business research. Turning to the Bible, we can find ample evidence for our Lord's concern for the poor. His mission is also identified with the task to uplift the humble and to feed the hungry with good things (Luke 1:53-54; Psalms 107:9). Who shall fill the hungry, and care for the poor? Though there are numerous attempts to answer poverty, poverty is still an identity for people especially in the third-world countries. For instance, in the 1990s, Africa, South of Sahara accounted for only about 1% of the total world trade. Such is a kind of place where social entrepreneurs and Christian missions are motivated to take venture.

In a place where people reside with poverty, missionaries and mission agencies in their attempt to integrate economic enterprises, they become part of a movement in social entrepreneurship that exhibits the concept of 'doing good' as described in the letter to Titus, "Our people must learn to devote themselves to doing what is good, in order that they may provide for daily necessities and not live unproductive lives" (Titus 3:14, NIV). The purpose of this chapter is to ground social entrepreneurship in the world of Christian thought and practice. This chapter will begin by setting out the missiological foundations, and then explore how these stories have shaped our understanding of Christian mission from the grand narratives.

2.1. Holistic Missional Approach

Holistic mission stems from a vertical relationship with God and horizontal relationship with men. It has as its concern an all-inclusive reaching out of an individual, group, and nation with an intent to proclaim the power of the gospel. The gospel action in holistic mission is carried out with a realization of the dynamic power of the gospel for spiritual, social, economic and even environmental transformation.

2.1.1. The Biblical Grand Narratives

Redemption in the Bible is associated with the transformation of the totality of creation, and salvation is viewed not as separate from creation. Creation itself is part of the redemptive program of God. Salvation is not about becoming a religious person, nor is it a state of complete detachment from the world. Rather a converted person, or 'new creation' are set as salt and light of this world. Becoming salt and light can be achieved in its fullest sense when we also direct our concern towards the things that are impacting the society. The good works for which God prepared in advance for us (Eph. 2:10) helps us to consider the fact that God's mission is not only a 'talking business' but also a 'doing business.' Mission is a God centered pragmatic movement for the entire cosmos. God's intention is not only to save the souls but "to reconcile to himself all things, whether things on earth or things in heaven" (Colossians 1:20). When we reconcile with God then His purpose becomes ours, and His mission or intention becomes ours.

The course of cosmic existence is for the glory of God, wherein the Triune God was actively participating in the creation. Paul reminds us that Christ was the agent of creation (Col. 1:16) and through Him was made the universe (Heb. 1:2). Creation is the handwork of God meant to proclaim His majesty and glory, but sin distorted this purpose and the power of darkness is hovering over creation. The power of darkness fills the earth with all sorts of greed, hatred, jealousy, selfishness, perversion, murder, violence, and name it. This is the holistic mission to which we are called to, and one which we will overcome under the Lordship of Christ (John 1:10, John 1:17, John 16:33).

2.1.2. The Creation Stories

There is plethora of creation account and rejoinders to various criticisms. The account of creation narrative is not settled even among the Christian scholars, but one thing is for certain, that God is He who created the whole universe. The entire cosmic plan springs from God, and He is the Grand Designer.

Creation is *ex-nihilo* "out of nothing." The use of 'create' in Genesis 1:1 is used in a manner pointing to something God does continually. God is continually active in the process of creating, and creating depends on His creative activity. It is God who sustains us. This statement can be anchored by the activity of divine sustenance when He feeds the Israelites with manna unceasingly for forty years, and leading them one step at a time. An important component of God's creation account is that God also cares for His creation, and His creation of the world is a gift to us; a representation that we are to engage in this world; and that this world matters to God. There are two creation stories.

a) The First Creation Story (Gen. 1:1-2:3)

The idea behind the first story is that God created the world in six days and took rest on the seventh day. The main phrase "and God said…" is repeatedly used and there is a harmonious perfection at the completion of creation. The earth was initially unsuitable place for mankind, being filled with darkness, formless and empty. But, upon completion, it was affirmed by God that it was good. God gave man a suitable place to live in and hence blessed them to fill and subdue the earth; and to rule over other creations (Gen. 1:28). This divine ordinance to mankind as steward of the earth allows us to consider the fact that we are connected to creation. For instance, we cannot ask God to do farming for us, but only that He will bless our hands and products. This honour of stewardship is to be carried out with the purpose to glorify God. So, whatever we did on earth has unique relation to the supremacy and glory of God. This is why the idea of social entrepreneurship lies in the foundation of our understanding God's own nature and character. A Social Entrepreneur following this mandate and God given example seen in the Grand Narrative will want to create sustainable ventures in broken places where no one else wants to invest their economic resources.

b) The Second Creation Story (Gen. 2:4-25)

The biblical passage to this second story of creation narrates the birth of man from dust, his placement in the Garden, and his responsibility "to work it and to take care of it." The honour was given to Adam of naming the animals (2:20). God wants us to participate, for His glory, in the engagement of our creativity to bring order, unity, peace, redemption, and prosperity on earth where we are dwelling.

2.1.3. The Fall of Mankind

Genesis 3 narrates the disobedience of man, and the judgment of God that befalls humankind. One of the major consequence of this disobedient act was the inability of Adam and Eve 'to work, create, sustain and care for the creation. Their disobedience distorted the creation mandate (Gen. 3:17-19).

The perverted state of human condition subsequent the fall, working the earth (or man's relationship to creation) took on a new shape. Instead of finding joy in the stewardship role of keeping the earth, man is now exposed to the penalty of hard labor. Working becomes a reminder of our brokenness and sins; a demeaning experience and a place of continual failure; no longer a place where we find our dignity. The depraved communication between humanity and creation no longer provides satisfaction but increase greed, pride, unhealthy competition, oppression, etc. Restoration of the joyous and fulfilling relationship with creation itself is part of the redemptive program, at the heart of mission, and a challenge for social entrepreneurs.

Due to the fall, there is now a wall of separation between God and his created mankind. Being separated from God, man began to wander away from God farther and farther until he became no longer accountable to God, or is almost completely lost. Due to his failure to acknowledge God's authority, man took matters in his own hand, act on his own free will and did whatever his heart so longs for. Once detached from a relationship with God, man eventually lived his life under the influence of Satan, the master of perversion. The aim of Satan is to disturb the order of creation, disturb peace, inflict misapprehension, and harbor chaos. The effect of sin brought upon a curse on the entire creation, and the ecosystems itself had suffered. Genesis 3:17-19 reads, "*Cursed is the ground because of you; through painful toil you will eat of it all the days of your life. It will produce thorns and thistles for you and you will eat the plants of the field. By the sweat of your brow you will eat your food until you return to the ground since from it you were taken, for dust you are and to the dust you will return.*"

It is a normal thing for a sinful man to disturb the ecosystems by using harmful materials. Fertilizers and chemicals were used in farming that depletes minerals in soil. Poisons were used for fishing, and harmful and poisonous chemicals were employed to meet certain needs of humanity. Trees were cut down mercilessly without any consideration of replacement. Everything inside the creation has been violated and disturbed. This results in ecological disorientation, and the balance of nature gets disturbed. Sin even destroys a relationship of an individual with that of the other.

Despite all these, the earth and everything in it including all who live in it are still the Lord's. The effects of sin do not belittle nor diminish the sovereignty of God, nor His power to salvation. Rather, it is the desire of God for a complete restoration, His heartbeat, the redemption of cosmos. The Edenic cosmic plan of God is characteristically a sustaining one. Joy, peace, security, health and wealth, were all but sustained by the presence of God and His fellowship with creation. Mission is the restoration of this relationship and communion.

It is within this landscape of a sin infested society a mission venture is launched with social entrepreneurship as a tool, but with the hope of a certain God who is still sovereign. The idea of Social Entrepreneurship as described in previous chapters with the framework of risk taking, innovation, and creating sustainable, humanitarian, profit making ventures is very much parallel to the Christian Missional approach which is in accordance with God's desire.

2.1.4. The Redemptive Plan of God

The brokenness of mankind was exacerbated further into three magnitudes: *The Death of Abel* (enmity between men), *The Flood* (enmity with nature), and *The Tower of Babel* (enmity with God).

Sin introduced enmity, a substance which was absent in the pre-fall. At the functional crux of creation is 'fellowship.' Between mankind, with nature, and with God. The highest purpose of mankind is to enjoy God and be in a fellowship with Him. This unique relation of God and man will follow 'the promise of God to bless all inhabitants of the earth,' and 'the obedience of man to God.' The post narrative account of the fall evidently display a lump of hope, a divine favor in a sinful darkened world. This evidence of God's promise can be glimpsed in the covenant of God with Noah and Abraham. Thus, despite the fall, God is still showing His loving intention for humanity and the entire cosmos. In the midst of a world that so often fails to reflect God's desire of *shalom*, God calls His people to form an obedient community of servants to the rest of creation. God's ultimate plan is to restore humanity and all creation into the new heaven and new earth, through the redemption of Jesus Christ on the cross, by paying the ransom for many which means all the descendants of Adam will be restored again through the death and the resurrection of Christ.

2.1.5. Covenantal Promises

The Adamic covenant assures God's blessings and allows Adam to become fruitful and multiple. However, disobedience to God lost Adam the privilege to work with the Lord in the Garden of Eden. There is thus a wall of separation between God and mankind. Yet, God still showed His grace and provided for them a way to salvation through Jesus Christ. This proclamation is stated in Genesis 3:15 also referred to as the *proto-evangelion* (the first gospel).

Taking into account that Noah became the progenitor of all mankind/humanity, it is safe to consider that Noahic covenant comprise all nations on earth. God is still the God of mankind and the only hope of salvation. It is well to keep in mind that Genesis 1-11 is the preface to the entire Bible and the foundation upon which the entirety of revelation is built. Genesis 9:10 reminds us that God's covenant, commitment, and promise is not only with all of humanity, but also with every living creature on earth. God is concerned not only towards humanity, but also preserving the earth from the destruction after the flood. The Noahic covenant provides the platform for the ongoing mission of God throughout the rest of human and natural history. After the flood, God renewed His promise to creation and human beings, and they were again sent under God's blessing to multiply and fill the earth. In Gen. 9:11, God promised that never again will there be a flood to destroy the earth. The Creation Mandate is renewed; the human task remains the same to practice authority over the rest of creation. God's purpose for creation is to preserve the earth with care and respect the life of every creature and human on the earth. That is the primary mission on the earth. The covenant of God with Noah effectively renewed this mission.

With Abraham, God made a covenant using the imperative 'Go.' The covenantal promise is set to be fulfilled through an act of going. This covenant served as the foundation upon which missions in the New Testament is built and engaged. The covenant in Genesis 12:1-3 is a covenantal promise of divine blessings, and the covenantal obligation of Abraham is obedience to God where divine purpose is to be accomplished through an act of Abraham going in response to

God's sending. We find this parallel in the New Testament when Jesus sends the church to all nations for the extension of His Kingdom.

2.1.6. Restorative Plan of God

Reading the biblical narratives, beginning from the first indication of human's sin and rebellion in Genesis 3-11, judgment with flood and the Noahic covenant, Abrahamic covenant in Genesis 12, emancipation from the Egyptian slavery, we can see the judgment of God mixed with mercy and the deliverance of Israelites and their being raised (by Yahweh) as a nation with a mission. Israel came into existence as a people with a mission entrusted to them from God for the sake of God's wider purpose of blessing the nations. Wright in *The Mission of God* stated, "in the midst of this people saturated with the scriptures, sustained by memory and hope, waiting for God, Jesus, the Davidic Messianic King steps-in with a mission. His mission was to restore Israel to Yahweh and also to be the agent of God's salvation reaching to the ends of the earth." Through obedience even unto death on the cross, the mission of God reached its climax; for God was restoring the world to Himself in Christ (2 Cor. 5:9). As Luke 24:45-47 indicates, Jesus entrusted the church with a mission directly rooted in His own identity with all of the same passion and victory of the crucified and risen Messiah. In an echo of Isaiah 43:10-12, Acts 1:8 declares that we as His disciples are His witnesses to the world. In addition to this, John 10:16 describes the universal mission of Christ as the Son of God who would die for the nations and gather all the scattered sheep into one fold.

2.2. Jubilee-*Future Hope*

The year of Jubilee occurred every 7 years in which God would extend His blessings and mercies, slaves and prisoners would be set free, debts would be forgiven, and the land was given a break from farming. Jubilee had two major focuses for the Israelites: *release or liberty* and *return or restoration* (Leviticus 25:10). Both of these terms can be easily applied strictly from economic provision of the Jubilee itself to a wider metaphorical application of the gospel. These economic terms became terms of hope and longing for the future and thus entered into prophetic eschatology. The hope of redemption and return for God's people are combined in the future vision of Isaiah 35, set alongside the equally dramatic hope of the transformation of nature. Most clearly of all, Isaiah 61 uses Jubilee images to portray the person anointed by the Lord to evangelize the poor, to proclaim liberty to the captives, and to announce the year of the Lord's favor.

The "Nazareth Manifesto" (Luke 4:16-30) is also a vivid support for this concept. It is the closest Jesus comes to a personal mission statement quoting directly from Isaiah 61, which was strongly influenced by Jubilee concept. Most commentators observe this Jubilee background as the prophetic test to Jesus' use of it. It clearly builds a holistic dimension into the mission that Jesus sets out for himself by reading this scripture and claiming to be its fulfillment.

2.3. The Cross - *the Path Towards New Heaven and New Earth*

> Revelation 21:1-4 *"Then I saw "a new heaven and a new earth," for the first heaven and the first earth had passed away, and there was no longer any sea. I saw the Holy City, the New Jerusalem, coming down out of heaven from God, prepared as a bride beautifully dressed for her husband. And I heard a loud voice from the throne saying, "Look! God's dwelling place is now among the people, and he will dwell with them. They will be his people, and God himself will be with them and be their God. 'He will wipe every tear from their eyes. There will be no more death' or mourning or crying or pain, for the old order of things has passed away."*

The cross is central to God's mission. It is divine intent that sin be punished and sinners forgiven; death be destroyed and eternal life granted; to defeat the power of evil and remove the barriers between Jews and Gentiles; and that enemies be reconciled. The redemptive program of God included the reconciliation of God with creation. These mission of God was fulfilled in the cross. The cross became an unavoidable cost of God's total mission. The fulfillment of the cross was seen in the person of Christ and his suffering where Christ submit to the will and mission of God, i.e. a cosmic redemption. Jesus taught that "at the resurrection people will neither marry nor be given in marriage" (Matthew 22:30) and in Revelation we are told that there will be no temple in New Jerusalem (Revelation 21:22). Jesus promised a second coming and our reconciliation with the Father. In that day, there will no longer be a need for religion, capitalism, businesses, or social entrepreneurship because Jesus will fulfill every need.

2.4. Social Entrepreneurship as Model for Holistic Mission

There can be plethora of models adopted for missions, but of these, social entrepreneurship stood out, perhaps as the most significant model for missions considering its analogous structure with the Grand Narratives. Following are models after which social entrepreneurship must be shaped:

a) Understanding the Heart of God for Creation

It does not take a man to be a Christian to esteem the teachings and accept the principles in the Bible. Many organizations or social entrepreneurs, regardless of their religious convictions embrace biblical principles in developing their strategic and creative social endeavors. Gandhi for instance took into account many moral and ethical standards of the Bible in his political struggle for Indian independence. In fact, his movement was motivated largely by the standard of Jesus.

The narratives of the Bible follows the fall of humanity, the plan of God for restoration, His redemptive program through Israelites, through Jesus and finally through the Church. This is the mission narrative which has been followed through Genesis to revelation. It is thus imperative that a social entrepreneurship be rooted in this mission narratives. Furthermore, this approach takes into account that people are spiritual, social and bodily beings made to live in relationship with God, with their neighbors, and with God's creations. Consequently, it presupposes that it is required to take care of the spiritual well-being of an individual with regard for his or her personal relationships and position in society and in the world.

Holistic Missions is therefore an approach that focuses on the formation of God-fearing people who understand themselves to be stewards of creation, to live selfless lives, and fulfill their God-given callings and vocation in the world. These people then understand how to give and receive and love, and are people who "hunger and thirst for justice," living as "peacemakers" (Matthew 5:6, 9).

The Material World Matters to the Creator

It is impossible to overlook the importance of the material world in God's agenda. The heavens and the earth, and all the things in it declare the glory of God. When our Creator designed people to be fruitful and multiply this included basic necessities and material needs being met. "Food that nourishes, roofs that hold out the rain, shade that protects us from the heat of the sun – these are all part of God's good design. When businesses produce material things that enhance the welfare of the community, they are engaged in work that matters to God." Thus, the material world matters to God.

Humans Beings are Called to Steward God's Creation

God created heaven and earth, living and non-living things on the earth, and He created human beings to enjoy His creation as stewards who have fellowship with God. As the Psalmist reminds us "The earth is the LORD's, and everything in it, the world, and all who live in it. (Psalm 24:1-2)." This is not to say that Adam and Eve randomly experienced God's benefits. They were given a role to play. We can identify this role as one of stewards. A steward is "a person who manages another's property or financial affairs; one who administrates anything as the agent of another." Human beings were called stewards of God's creation on God's behalf. "*The Lord God took the man and put him in the Garden of Eden to work it and take care of it*" (Genesis 2:15). The first step in stewardship occurs when entrepreneurs or businessmen recognize that their businesses do not belong to them but rather to God. Social Entrepreneurs understand the concept of stewardship which is why they invest profits back into the community for the benefit of others. They do not keep the profits for themselves or share among the shareholders.

Human Beings are Made in the Image of God

Human beings are created in the image of God, (Genesis 1:26-27, 2 Corinthians 4:4, Colossians 1:15). Being made in the image of God points to the fact that the image bearer plays a role in revealing the essence of the other. That is why we reflect His character. Since God is the Creator and creates out of nothing (ex nihilo), human creativity is always derivative and is always derived from the work of the Creator. Creating reflects God's image. To innovate and bring into being new things and new ways of doing things reflects the Creator's image. In a same manner, Social Entrepreneurs engage in creative, meaningful work that grows out of relationship or empathy and give back to the community.

b) Create as the Triune God Creates

By virtue of our creative endowment by a creating God, we are expected to achieve an end not of self-glorifications, fame, power, statue, success, but to the fulfillment of God's mission by the restoration of a chaotic world. Keller contrasted the Biblical creation narrative with that of other ancient cultures and creation beliefs. In most stories, the world comes about as a result of violence between gods. The biblical God has no rivals who could make him fight. God wasn't forced to create, nor did God do so by accident. He created since it is His nature.

c) Creating for Others

Those who create like God do so for the sake of others. The triune God is always doing things for others. God creates so others will have space and share His good and know Him. Human creators should follow His example, since we are His image. Social Entrepreneurs have a goal to be Christ-like in creating and innovating for the goal of others needs being met.

d) Taking Risks in Creating

Those social entrepreneurs who create like God know the risk and the cost. God was not surprised by humanity's fall in Genesis, and God knew that He would take on flesh and go to hell to bring about the salvation of humanity. Likewise, social entrepreneurs create knowing there will be risk, and yet they pursue new ventures for the sake of others to follow the example of God the Father.

e) Creates Knowing the Worth

"God didn't just perform one great act of entrepreneurship." There was a second act described in 2 Corinthians 5:17-19, "*God was in Christ reconciling the world to himself.*" In order to create a new humanity of reconciled sisters and brothers in His Son, God was willing to create anew. In the same way, entrepreneurs create in full knowledge of the difficulties possible but also in full confidence that the reward will be worth it. Keller explains that Christian entrepreneurs have a leg up on secular social entrepreneurship because if Christians fail to achieve good work through their ventures, God sees their efforts and the intention of their hearts. Either way, blessings come as Christians put their trust in God.

The Work in the Garden Was Incomplete

In the Garden of Eden we see that Adam and Eve were assigned specific responsibilities. They were asked to "subdue" and "rule" over creation, and to be fruitful and multiply (Genesis 1:28). They were given opportunity to name the animals and classify them bringing order to creation (Genesis 2:19-20). They were called to take care of the earth (Genesis 2:15). "Their good work fortifies their identity and solidifies the satisfaction within. In contrast, bad work breeds bad reputation and burdensome guilt within. Social entrepreneurs recognize the importance of striving to make this world a better place to live". We see in Genesis that Adam and Eve only partially completed their jobs in the garden, due to the fall, their assignments were left unfinished and brought future curses.

2.5. Venture to Overcome the Fall

The challenges facing today's corporations can be a crisis for possible closure, extreme emphasis on profit (earning money) at the cost of social exploitation. Such motive is a distortion of the primary purpose and more importantly dishonoring God. The motive behind social entrepreneurship is not profit-oriented, nor is it concerned with the exploitation of others. It is built upon the inspiration of building societies. It moves with empathy to bring change, and does not focus on personal or selfish gains. Social entrepreneurship otherwise is as good as dead. Social entrepreneurship is to be considered non-functional unless it has the right motive.

Tuning social entrepreneurship towards the right direction requires it to be rooted in the Cross, where Christ proclaimed victory over death and sin. Social entrepreneurship is a venture of resurrection, a proclamation of victory in the sense that it lends hands towards the downtrodden and the oppressed who are considered as nothing. It is in the undertaking of social entrepreneurship where we can witness the resurrected power of the Cross, and the assurance of power that enables Christians to live the value of Kingdom in the midst of a fallen world. It is the space where we could taste the power of the Holy Spirit where we are called and enabled to bring evidence of God's triumph into the world. "*You will receive power when the Holy Spirit comes upon you; and you will be my witness in Jerusalem, and in all Judea, and Samaria, and to the ends of the earth*" (Acts 1:8). We testify to God's victory, not only in words, but by deeds that are evidence of God's justice and righteousness. "*For the kingdom of God is not a matter of talk but of power*" (1 Corinthians 4:20).

A popular business maxim reads, "Good ethics is good business." True, but it does not imply the fact that not all business enterprises are based and built upon on Kingdom principles and values. Social entrepreneurship, however, is based on Kingdom's principles and values, and functions in parallel with biblical principles. Social entrepreneurs operate in a fallen world where divine intervention and victory is assured but not fully evident. This led to a realization that the venture of social entrepreneurship is marked with several risks. For these facts, it becomes imperative that the undertakings of social entrepreneurship be carried out with prayer and divine wisdom. The focus of this venture is always about helping the needy and the poor. Thus, the task of social entrepreneurs is a challenging one especially since it can be called as calling of a higher standard.

However, hard and challenging a task it may seem, social entrepreneurship is nonetheless glorious, for it is a participation in the creative and redemptive work of God. And for the reason that social entrepreneurship operated under the Kingdom script, it is counted as a privilege and a satisfying endeavor.

2.6. Strive Towards Redemption and Restoration

The redemptive and restorative program of God invites us to participate in the world. The mission of God is never detached from the society. It sees the people, not only in terms of their need for spiritual emancipation but also social liberation. And that is a calling unto which Christians are called: *to become a social agents of God on earth.* By this virtue, social entrepreneurship becomes a tool and opportunity for social transformation. The reconciliation and redemption of the fallen world encompass aspects of social well-being.

Just as the cross of Christ actuated the power of resurrection, social entrepreneurship aims towards social resurrection, that is, resurrection from social oppression, poverty, etc. In this sense, social entrepreneurship is an attempt to reinforce the resurrection intended by God. Just as Jesus defeated the power of Satan through resurrection, social entrepreneurship is a venture to ensure victory over social evils.

Social entrepreneurship therefore is *liberative.* The Exodus account entails the liberation of the Israelites from the Egyptian bondage. The liberation of God's people is not merely a political emancipation or declaration of independence. It is also social, economic, physical and spiritual. Based on this narrative, recent years have witnessed an emergence of several liberation theologies such as Feminist theology, Black theology, Tribal theology, Dalit theology, and so on. These are evident to show that God is concerned not only of our spiritual salvation but also social salvation. God is concern for the entire human race and the entire creation. All are included under His program of redemption and restoration. In fact, creation itself will be restored when all is completed. The narrative account of the rich man and Lazarus in Luke 16:19-31 is a clear depiction that God is in the business of crushing the disparity between peoples (social disparity-rich and poor, black and white, Dalit and non-Dalit, male and female, tribal and non-tribal etc), liberation of the creation (Rom 8:19).

Social entrepreneurship takes into consideration the heartbeat of God for His creation. It is a liberative venture, and an attempt to provide a sustainable solution to social problems. It is a noble act of catering the individual needs of the people where they could venture into a meaningful, creative, and life giving work. It is a social mission venture programmed to participate in the redemptive plan of God.

2.7. Venture for Peace with Nature and Humanity

Social entrepreneurship is a venture to restore relationships in all dimensions. It is a shalom project of reconciling creation with God, and in the process answers the problem of social issues. It provides a sustainable relationship between humanity and creation, and God. As such, the venture of social entrepreneurship requires that they remain conscious of their environment and consumers. The main purpose in terms of business will be sustainability. Certain businesses should not harm anyone involved in the process of pursuing godly objectives and seeking profitably.

God created a perfect world for us (Genesis 1:31), but mankind sinned. We now see the consequences of our sin. The fall definitely caused an enmity between humanity and nature. For centuries, Christian mission was focused on saving souls and meeting human needs, but it completely neglected being good stewards where God has placed us. We read in the Bible that after the Fall the earth produced thorns and thistles (Genesis 3:18). Now we are seeing what we did not see in the past, enmity between creation and man. If this continues, there will be many more natural disasters unlike anything human history has ever seen or heard. Mankind, made in God's own image (Genesis 1:26), is given the command to exercise stewardship over the rest of His creation (the earth and its creatures; Genesis 1:28, 2:15; Psalm 115:16). God requires us to responsibly look after His creation and not simply do as we please. Our mission is to obey Jesus' command to be responsible stewards until His return (Luke 12:41-48), as we wait for the final redemption (Romans 8:20-22). Similarly, the Bible talks about how the land suffers (Jeremiah 12:4) and mourns (Hosea 4:1-3) because of the sin of God's people.

It communicates how the land 'vomits' unfaithful Israel due to sin (Leviticus 18:25-28), and how the creation groans (Romans 8:19-22) as it awaits redemption. Biblically, human behavior indeed affects the whole earth – including the climate.

Just as God is working to bring peace, so should Social Entrepreneurs, as it is biblically justified; it should be an integral part of missions. Our work should be an expression of our worship to God and His wonderful plan of redemption through Jesus Christ. Therefore, our ministry of reconciliation is a matter of joy and hope, and we should care for creation even when it is not in crisis. Christian Social Entrepreneurs should join in this important call to bring peace between nature and humanity as it may help in the healing of the land.

Today, creation is groaning because of the harm we have inflicted on it, and it waits to be "*liberated from the bondage to decay*" (Romans 8:21-22). Remarkably, creation is also "*waiting in eager expectation for the children of God to be revealed.*" In other words, creation is waiting for the worldwide churches to recover its calling to reflect God's image through godly and just care for God's world. As we step out to do this, bringing hope based on God's commitment to creation and the knowledge that one day everything in heaven and on earth will be once again under Jesus's authority" (Ephesians 1:10).

Conclusion

In the light of the above discussions on the Grand Biblical narratives, it becomes clear that God is actively participating in the redemption of this world, that He loves the world, gave it to us as gift and appointed us as caretakers of creation. This mission of stewardship is made possible through our relationship with Christ despite our inability to fulfill the cosmic mission task for the reason of our perverted state.

It is also interesting to note that in the attempt to place social entrepreneurship in a stewardship task, we could derive a unique framework for entrepreneurship model. This model is shaped from a kingdom perspective detached from the dichotomy of church and state, or the exclusivity of mission mandate for social welfare and promotion.

We are now under the New Covenant since Christ has become the atonement for our sins. That means followers of Christ are dead to sin and alive to God (2 Corinthians 4:7-18). It means we have become the slaves of righteousness (2 Corinthians 4:7-18). We are God's handiwork, created in Christ Jesus to do good works, which God prepared in advance for us to do (Ephesians 2:10). That good work is creative, redemptive, and restorative, work to undo what was caused by the Fall in Genesis 3:6. Social Entrepreneurs understand the need of the hour for humanity and creation. They walk closely to the heart of God to spread Good News for the whole creation.

Countless possibilities can be made if enough ingenuity, compassion, and innovation are applied. They say that man cannot live on bread alone, but neither can he live on faith alone. Finding that balance with the social mission of charities, both secular and religious; the brainpower of academia; and the efficiency and entrepreneurship of business leaders could go a long way toward creating sustainable communities around the world. In finding this great balance, we will live lives of great respect, dignity, and with greater purpose. We will not only generate economic stability for us and for local people, but we will also be doing God's mission through evangelism and through the creation mandate.

Chapter 3

Biblical Perspectives on Social Entrepreneurship

The Bible is filled with an overarching account of the fall, God's promise and His acts of restoration. Since the beginning, it is evident that God is continually and actively working so as to bring His creation to Himself and to restore them to their former self (which is the original plan God has for humankind, i.e., the unfallen state). It is in this program that we are invited to participate. This participation is the precursor of our following of Christ as our Lord and Savior. The realization of Christ as our Savior inaugurates our participation in God's kingdom plan. Our role entailed in this participation is to reveal the nature and character of God. The heart of God is to bring about the restoration of humanity to Himself, so that God may be able to bring peace among humans, and between humans and nature. It is then the double task of social entrepreneurship to bring restoration among men and between men and nature.

Social entrepreneurs have a purpose beyond profit, and that could certainly come from spiritual beliefs. But, the vast majority of social entrepreneurs had traditional motives, i.e., they wanted to work for themselves or sell a product or service that would earn them a good living. On the contrary, social entrepreneurs move with empathy, since their entire intention for creating venture is to redeem those people who are neglected by our society or by the government and restore them and make them sustainable out of love since God's creation is an expression of His love only.

Hunger, poverty, environmental degradation, economic instability, unemployment, chronic diseases, drug addiction, and war, for example, persist in spite of the analytical ability and technical brilliance that have been directed towards eradicating them. No one deliberately creates those problems, no one wants them to persist, but they persist nonetheless. That is because of our sinful nature, such as greed, selfishness, and cruelty.

Mission has been progressive or it has been done in most cases out of necessity or out of need of the context. Hence compartmentalized approach should not be considered inherently an evil, rather should be acknowledged as a limited approach. However, the gospel should approach being creative to redeem and to restore, what was brought by 'fall' which we can see throughout the Old and the New Testaments both.

3.1. Old Testament Narratives

The entire narrative of the Old Testament is governed by a cycle of *problems, solutions,* and *restoration.* God is the solution to the problems or crisis of Israelites, and a restorative power that reinstate the Israelites to a state where there is sustainable freedom and liberty in relationship with YHWH.

The flood narrative (Gen. 6:9-9:7) shows the judgment of God mixed with mercy. The crisis of sin leads to punishment, but the salvation of the righteous (Noah and his family). The narrative is also a clear indication of God's concern for the entire creation. Noah was commanded to build an ark, not for himself and his family alone, but for all creatures. This portrays God's concern for the well-being of the ecosystem. More interestingly, sabbath was not only ordained for humans but for animals (Exodus 20:10, 23:12), and for the land too (Exodus 23:10-11). We can also see the prohibitions against waste (Deut. 20:19-20); land's suffering due to impurities (Lev. 18:24-30); laws for 'Goring Ox' (Exodus 21:28-29); enemy's Ox or Donkey (Exodus 23:4-5); sensitivity to animals' feelings (Exodus 23:19); giving helping hands to neighbours' animals (Deut. 22:1-4); prohibitions against causing pain to animals (Deut. 22:6-7). All of these passages show God's concern for animals and the birds of the air, including the whole earth. After the flood crisis, and the solution of the ark, God restored His creation.

The exodus narrative begins with the birth of Moses in a state of crisis (bondage of Israelites under the Egyptians). There are evident social disruptions where we can see the Israelites as an oppressed class, and Egyptians as the oppressors. Reading from a social entrepreneurship perspective, the ten plagues upon the Egyptians can be symbolized as a cause for their oppressiveness. The Israelites could not bear the pain they suffered under their taskmasters and thus called upon the Lord for intervention. It can be said that the acts of human beings had an adverse effect that summoned natural calamities.

3.2. New Testament Narratives

In New Testament times, social entrepreneurship was a key to the spread of the gospel and social justice in the early church of the Roman Empire. There was no concept of charity to the poor in Roman culture. However, by caring for those in need who were outside of their own families and communities, Christians acted as social innovators. The statement by Roman Emperor Julian (4th century AD) reflects the power of social innovation in spreading the gospel: "[Christianity] has been specially advanced through the loving service rendered to strangers, and through their care for the burial of the dead. It is a scandal ... that the ... Galileans care not only for their own poor but for ours as well; while those who belong to us look in vain for the help that we should render them."

All the four gospels come to an end with the commissioning of the disciples on a mission to the world "Go therefore and make disciples of all nations.... And remember, I am with you always to the end of the age" (Matthew. 28:19-20). "Go into all the world and proclaim the good news to the whole creation" (Mark 16:15). "Repentance and forgiveness of sin is to be proclaimed in his name to all nations, beginning from Jerusalem ... I am sending upon you what my father promised ....power from on high" (Luke 24:44-49). "As the father has sent me, so I send you. When he had said this, he breathed on them", "receive the Holy Spirit..." (John 20:21-23). However, sending for what? Sending to preach the Good News of salvation to those who are lost, in this world, like lost sheep (Luke 15:1-7) and lost coin (Luke 15:8-10). All of these scripture send us for mission, mission of redemption and restoration.

The narrative of the Good Samaritan also portrays that giving and receiving mercy transcends national, racial, or religious barriers. There is also ample evidence in the New Testament where we can see women being given dignity and respect, to people who are culturally and socially looked down by the society. A good example will be that of the tax collector or the prostitute woman.

However, social entrepreneurs go along with these people in our community too, to uplift them and help them regain their dignity and respect just as Luke portrait Jesus in the Gospel of Luke. Through the Gospel, Jesus was portrayed as a friend to those who are marginalized by society, such as tax collector, prostitute women, and the poor. Luke further explained that the problem of poverty lies in the Christian *koinonia*, where Christian communities shared their wealth with the poor as a redeemed community. That can happen through deliverance by the power of Holy Spirit in Christ Jesus. Such as Social Entrepreneurs, they do good works not with compulsion but with an inner motive, which actually becomes the driving force for them to carry on this good work tirelessly. They are motivated to involve themselves in the community who are pushed out or neglected by the government, through innovative and sustainable ventures.

John 9:1-17 is another narration on a blind man. Being blind or blindness is an identity, and the blinds were socially ostracized during those days. According to the purity system, disabled people were considered as sinners and they were looked down and considered untouchable. They were not permitted to enter into the Jerusalem temple (2 Sam. 5:8, Lev. 21:18; 22:22). However, before Jesus heals this blind man, He himself had a conflict with these religious leaders who wanted to kill Jesus, in the time of Tabernacle. It was in that context, this Blind man encountered Jesus. Jesus explained the new perspective about this man and tells why he was blind. Here Jesus' perspective was very different from that of His disciple. Jesus took an initiative; he takes the mud and his saliva, puts it in the eye of that blind man and healed him, even breaking the Sabbath law. He was willing to be treated as an unclean or a sinner through the act of healing this blind man.

Jesus can be seen here as a Social Entrepreneur. Jesus combines the element of the earth or the resources that were easily available and mixed with his saliva which has the part of his own body or the resources he already had. He created mud and applied on blind man's eye and asked him to participate in the healing process, go and wash in the pool of Siloam. The act of making mud with the saliva and applying it on the eyes of the visually impaired destitute gave him a new life. The entire life of the formerly blind man was transformed with him gaining his sight. The man who was formerly born blind and used to sit and beg is now bold and courageous before all people. He was branded as a sinner and unclean, but now he is completely transformed by the intervention of Jesus with the co-operation of the element (Natural Resources) of the earth. Yet he is not accepted as a normal dignified human being. His past is brought out to haunt him and keep him in his oppressed state. Now he can stand on his own legs and fight his cause without the help of anyone else. John here presents the healed man defending himself and speaking with extraordinary courage. The formally blind man is empowered to face all the criticism and oppression from the Jewish leaders.

Jesus' partnership with the earth and its element is not for profit. His collaboration with nature is to make healing freely available in nature. Unlike the profit oriented partnership with nature, such as unbridled mining, which approaches nature and its resources for making a monetary gain, eventually doing harm to nature, Jesus' action is intended to cooperate with nature for bringing about liberation freely to a stigmatized person, that he can sustain by himself.

However, we can understand through this narrative, that we are interconnected with nature since we are made out of dust and the breath of God (Genesis 2:7). Through this passage, Jesus again demonstrates the relationship between dust, human beings and God for the wholeness of humanity.

3.3. Jesus as Social Entrepreneur

Christian social entrepreneurship is the creative answer for redemption and restoration in a place of crisis, and a venture through faith. This allows us to ponder on social entrepreneurship not only as a key to change in physical circumstances (of the downtrodden or vulnerable people in a community) but also a powerful tool for change and upliftment of a community. In this way, Jesus is seen as a social entrepreneur who presented Christianity as a new way of life and thinking. Jesus as a social entrepreneur challenged and altered the Graeco-Roman worldview of religion and life.

Jesus tackled major social issues during his time. He served people being a religious leader and taught people to love and serve one another. Now, Jesus includes all of us who accept him into his loving family for eternity by giving his life for our ransom (John 3:16). He made an ultimate sacrifice for the world, that he may change the destiny of this world. His death and resurrection caused a U-Turn in the lives of those that chose to follow him now and tomorrow.

Jesus never sought help from religious leaders nor from the officials, he solved his and people's problems by himself such as, he healed the sick (Matthew 4:23; Mark 7:30 Mark 10:45; Luke 6:6-10 Matthew 15:28-30; Matthew 8:4, he blesses (Mark 10:13; Luke 18:15 Matthew 19:13), he washes the feet of his disciples (John 13:1-17), he raises the dead (Mark 5:21-43; John 11:1-45, he feeds the masses (Matthew 14:13-21), and many others. He was doing all these to restore what was damaged by the Fall. He was in the mission of redemption and restoration. However, like every great Social Entrepreneur, Jesus started small and surrounded himself with few people who are willing to catch his vision and dream and are willing to take the risk along with him. However, the mission or movement which he began 2000 years ago still goes on. There are almost 2.2 billion people who follow his teachings and draw principles for their lives. Jesus paved the way and set the example for us as the Church to follow and to be the ultimate social entrepreneur. To this day, due to the profound impact that began when Jesus walked upon this earth, the world continues to yearn to know and to follow him. And we as Christians continue his social entrepreneurship, or mission, by getting involved in the work of redemption and restoration.

Conclusion

As we looked at social entrepreneurship through the Biblical perspective, and realized that social entrepreneurship is very much mission oriented since it reflects the heart of God through its venture. There are many Social Entrepreneurs around the world that are working in a various sectors such as Health, Education, Microcredit, Fair Trade, Human Rights and Social Justice, Disaster Relief and Rehabilitation, The Environment and The Restoration of a Sustainable Planet, and many other agents of change around the globe, and the number is growing. However, there are many Christian mission organizations which do charitable or philanthropic work since they can get charity easily from the people or churches in the name of mission work. There are more than 33,000 denominations in the world, most of them are dependent on charity. Since people's faith has drifted away from God and Christianity, they are not giving charity. There is no question that Christians are well-represented in the entrepreneurial community — a study from Baylor University found that entrepreneurs tend to be more likely to believe that God is personally responsive to them than others. However, when the authors of the study were asked if the entrepreneurs' faith explained the growing interest in social entrepreneurship, they replied that most entrepreneurs were generally motivated because they wanted to work for themselves to earn a good living; it was not about creating a social impact. Since the new generation is not really thinking about making a difference in the community and are just thinking about themselves and their family, the question is that who will think about making a difference in our society, city and in our country. Giving tracks, opening a hospital, opening a school, opening an orphanage, opening old an age home, are wonderful things but, we must run along with time. We must understand the heartbeat of God for today's situations.

However, Christian mission agencies or missionaries can develop Social Entrepreneurship as an alternative model for an innovative and sustainable Christian mission work in the realm of Health, Education, Microcredit, Fair Trade, Human Rights and Social Justice, Disaster Relief and Rehabilitation, The Environment and The Restoration of a Sustainable Planet, and many other agents of change; because social entrepreneurship encourages people to think about sustainability from several angles, including financial, social, and environmental which are often called the "triple bottom line." Social entrepreneurship could conceptually be one way to redeem and harness market-driven mechanisms for social good and encourage the private sector, which has the capital, to collaborate more deeply with the nonprofit sector, which has the keen understanding of social problems caused by Fall or Sin.

Chapter 4

Theological Reading of Social Entrepreneurship

Social entrepreneurship gains popularity and many organizations such as Ashoka, LifeBread, SariBari, Christian Help, Grameen Bank, all have adopted this model for an unattainable and long-lasting change. However, it has been our intention to understand social entrepreneurship in the light of Christian mission. Christian Social Entrepreneurship is the way to bring redemption (in the place of crisis) and restoration (sustainability) through creativity into a society for the common good, by introducing faith ventures which have Kingdom prospective.

Mission in its essence is a key to unlock the secrets of human existence, not a set of philosophical truths, nor recurring rituals or unchanging institutions. It is just a series of events unfolding in history: creation, fall, redemption, and glorification, which is the gospel of Jesus Christ. There are several ways to accomplish this mission task, and it is the purpose of this research to present 'social entrepreneurship' as one of such. We can take Christian social entrepreneurship as the process of pursuing innovative and sustainable solutions to social problems. It becomes imperative for

Christian leaders today to incorporate business with mission in order to impact the lives of people integrally or holistically. Mission is no longer about evangelization, but also for social transformation. Missions today is inclusive of three important aspects: *economic, social,* and *spiritual.*

4.1. Theological Consideration

The use of a parable in Luke 6:46-49 puts into perspective the significance of laying a solid, enduring foundation for our lives. The Biblical orientation is about the successful development of human Christian character that is reflective of the Gospel message; it is more about building up the body of Christ and the Kingdom of God here on Earth. We can see Tabitha in Acts 9:36-42 to illustrate this point. "In Joppa there was a disciple named Tabitha (in Greek her name is Dorcas); she was always doing good and helping the poor. About that time, she became sick and died, and her body was washed and placed in an upstairs room. Lydda was near Joppa; so when the disciples heard that Peter was in Lydda, they sent two men to him and urged him, "Please come at once!" Peter went with them, and when he arrived he was taken upstairs to the room. All the widows stood around him, crying and showing him the robes and other clothing that Dorcas had made while she was still with them. Peter sent them all out of the room; then he got down on his knees and prayed. Turning toward the dead woman, he said, "Tabitha, get up." She opened her eyes, and seeing Peter she sat up. He took her by the hand and helped her to her feet. Then he called for the believers, especially the widows, and presented alive them. This became known all over Joppa, and many people believed in the Lord" (New International Version).

The Scripture tells us that Tabitha was generously giving away her tunics and other clothing to the widows. This, however, is no reason to assume that her generosity extended only to that extent of giving tunics and clothing. Yet, it becomes more reasonable to assume that Tabitha's acts of kindness encompass a far greater work than a generous donation. Her actions and her helpful personality would have led her to many other acts of kindness to needy people also. People who have experienced suffering and difficult situations understand how hard that can be and how a small act of generous kindness can serve to fix that difficulty. However, we can be sure that Tabitha was not a very poor widow. She had the means to share generously with others; Tabitha reveals the heart of God towards needy people. This example can be used to show how God will bless (as He did Tabitha) those who are willing to help the downtrodden.

The notion that regular gainful employment ensures charitable activities and social responsibility on the part of the church still does not yet explicitly appear here. Yet, one should remember that and admonitions in 1 Thessalonians 4:11 "to work with your hands" comes under the category of "love of the brothers and sisters" (1 Thessalonians 4:9). However, the principle is formatted clearly in the later Letter to the Ephesians, which presumably was not written by Paul himself, but by one of his disciples. Here, the foundations of an "early Christian social ethics" are outlined for the first time in the history of Christianity. Ephesians 4:28 reads: "Thieves must give up stealing; rather let them labor and work honestly with their own hands, so as to have something to share with the needy." Accordingly, Christians must engage in a regular work in order to be able to share their earned income with others.

Being a follower of Christ we must help the poor to overcome poverty in their lives. "According to John, "If anyone has world's goods and sees his brother in need, yet closes his heart against him, how does God's love abide in him?" (1 John 3:17). In Galatians 2:10, Paul says, "they asked us to remember the poor, the very thing I was eager to do". We can also see this in Matthew 25:39-40, Acts 2:45, 4:35, Romans 12:13, 15:25-27, Eph. 4:28, Titus 3:14, Hebrew 13:16."

How should we open our hearts to the poor and to our brothers in need? Many are involved in short term solutions such as providing one meal or giving a small amount of money, but this is not enough for the needy to not beg again. All those things are good, but it is not a permanent and sustainable solution. Christian Social Entrepreneurship can be the best long term solution for those who want to provide sustainable solutions for the desperate and needy people in our society.

4.2. Manna Economy of Jesus

There is a sharp distinction between 'need' and 'want' in the words of Jesus Christ when he told them not to worry about what they will eat or drink (Matt. 6:25; Luke 12:22) since God will supply their needs just as He sustained Israelites in the wilderness (Exp. 16:4-5, 16-30). The intention here is to let the disciples understand that God will provide them their 'need for the day.' God supplies the birds who neither sow nor reap, and through this sustenance Jesus comforts the people that they should not be worried about tomorrow (Matt. 6:34). One good reason for this is seen in Genesis 41:47, so that we can share but not store more than what we need. God doesn't want us to like the foolish man mentioned in Luke 12:16-20.

Social entrepreneurship at the hands of mission is no longer about accumulation of wealth or desire for profits/benefits, rather a service to God. An entrepreneurship objective of generating wealth is set against divine principles, but the entrepreneurship we insist on introducing and implementing in mission is a production of sustainable economy that serves the needs of the society, and not the organization, company or whatsoever. This principle of serving is derived from the fact that God is the ultimate source of all things and He has given us resources, talents, and brains to produce and provide.

4.3. Characteristics of Christian Social Entrepreneurship

While Christian social entrepreneurship initially strives to accomplish social value and create incomes to cover its running costs, it has the tendency to operate like the traditional business enterprise - to achieve the highest commercial and service standards, with highest goals being serve and make a difference in the community.

Christian Social Entrepreneurship aims to achieve a sustainable economic standard by providing job opportunity, vocational training, and services. It is a venture which thinks outside the box and extended towards creating a privilege for the underprivileged who are deprived of their opportunity and redeem their social and economic status. A common social entrepreneurship philosophy follows, "that everyone and everything can make a positive difference to the community if given a second chance."

4.3.1. Overcoming "Greed"

Every enterprise or business undertaking wants 'profit.' Or to be more specific, personal and corporate gain driven by greed. Greed is an almost inevitable presence in all business enterprise. When Thomas Wolfe said, "you have reached the pinnacle of success as soon as you become uninterested in money, compliments, or publicity." Wolfe is implying that success is measured not by the quantity of your material or profit accumulation, but by our ability to overcome personal appetite. Human desires for fame and wealth has no limits, but it is also a remarkable reminder of how fallen we are. Greed is the cause of all economic disorder.

Yet, when we turn to the New Testament, we can find ample evidence of the need for 'generosity' or generous acts. The Scripture encourages its adherents towards a kingdom lifestyle of seeking desirable deeds performed in the lives of others, and not living our lives working for the 'unrighteous mammon' in a self-seeking and self-centered manner. It encourages us to put our ultimate trust in God, and be willing to demonstrate that trust through sacrificial giving. It encourages us to be wary of and wise about the fallen economic and political institutions of this world, and to do our best to disengage from their unethical practices. It encourages us to live a *koinonia* communal life. Greed is repeatedly warned as a soul-destroying force. According to Grudem, the goal of the Christian life is not prosperity, or happiness, but rather godliness and holiness, loving God and one's neighbor wholeheartedly.

The distinctive mark of the New Testament community is fellowship, *koinonia.* The *koinonia* (fellowship) is a family likeness structured with a deep sense of belongingness and love. It prompts the *koinonia* community to share everything they have, their wealth and material. No one is concerned of self, but of the welfare of others and the community as a whole. It is a community centered standard of fellowship. There was no master no slave but the community of brethren (Matthew 20:26, Philemon 1:16). In the community of brethren, the greed for possession and claim to the personal property comes to an end. The community of brethren proclaims the Kingdom of God through its way of life.

To have desires for material things, and to strive for temporal wealth are themselves not sinful. It is perfectly honorable to spare our strength for 'work' and accumulate wealth, but it is dishonorable in the sight of God when our means of achieving that end comes with a price of harming the cause of others. It dishonors God when our undertaking comes with a selfish motive and greed. To be greedy for temporal wealth and to make a 'mammon' of it is always wrong in every office, position and occupation. Money is like manure; it's not worth a thing unless it's spread around encouraging young things to grow (Thornton Wilder). People of God must know how to earn and spend for the purpose of God rather than selfish gain.

4.3.2. Celebrating the Jubilee in Christ

Pope Benedict XVI recently captured this idea of giving, specifically when he was talking about giving our lives to Christ. And once we give our life to Christ everything changes. He says: "Are we not perhaps all afraid in some way? If we let Christ enter fully into our lives, if we open ourselves totally to Him, are we not afraid that He might take something away from us? No! If we let Christ into our lives, we lose nothing, nothing, absolutely nothing of what makes life free, beautiful and great...When we give ourselves to Him, we receive a hundredfold in return. Yes, open, open wide the doors to Christ – and you will find true life."

Jesus, time and again, reiterated in many of His teachings, particularly through the parables, that the only proper use of wealth is in the care of the poor (Luke 18:18-30, Mark 10:17-31, Matt 19:16-30, Luke 16:19-31, Luke 12:13-21, etc.). Since God has a special interest for the poor, destitute, and needy, so should we as the children of God.

Christian Social Entrepreneurs celebrate their freedom in Christ by being an agent of God, by sharing their time, talent, and treasure to bring lost people back to God. Therefore, if anyone is in Christ, is a new creation, the old has gone, the new has come (2 Corinthians 5:17). They do this because they recognize that this is the heart of God, and they recognize who they are in Christ. Jesus said, "Watch out! Be on your guard against all kinds of greed; life does not consist in an abundance of possessions (Luke 12:15)" Psalm 119:36, Jeremiah 22:17, Ezekiel 33:31, Luke 12:16, 1 Timothy 6:6, Psalm 62:10, But "This is how it will be with whoever stores up things for themselves but is not rich towards God (Luke 12:21). Christian Social Entrepreneurs understand that whatever they have is a gift given by God and they are just "stewards".

4.4. Social Entrepreneurship as Kingdomnomic Ventures

What is the Biblical image of 'business'? When we try to understand the very word 'business,' our minds are overwhelmingly painted with images of a lavish lifestyle, marked with distinctive objects of material things such as beautiful houses, cars, hotels, money etc. Business is almost always associated with material surplus. However, the Bible has a rather astonishing image of business.

A considerable number of people can be named as business persons. For instance, Lydia, the first convert to Christ in Europe was a 'merchant' by profession. Her business was "dealer in purple cloth" (Acts 16:14). Essentially Lidia was a business owner who earlier produced and sold a fine fabric that was in demand in her day, though her career was not specifically praised but was not criticized either.

What was the profession of Peter, James, and John? These men were involved in the business of fishing. We might quickly think that they left. However, it does not tell that they used to ply their trade on occasion, nor there is any implication that they left their business because it was wrong. They had to become a student at that point. They were called to become a disciple of Jesus at that point. It is like a person is called to become a full-time pastor. It is their call to do a pastoral job. However, this disciple continued fishing in times of need (John 21). And, they still owned their boat and net at a sea shore.

There are other people in the bible who were businessmen, such as Philemon, who was rich and knew how to put his wealth to good use; supporting the ministry, refreshing the saints, and letting local Church meet in his home. Amos, David, and Jethro (Exodus 18) were shepherds. Luke was a physician. What about Paul and

Jesus? Paul comes from a business background of "tent-making" (Acts 18:3), and he practiced during his mission trips too. Through his business, he was self-sustained in his mission and could even provide for others who were in need (1 Cor. 9: 6-18). Through business, he was able to relate with businessmen such as Pricilla and Aquila (Acts 18:1-3). At the same time, we can see our Lord Jesus, he was directly involved with his father's business of carpentry, where they made tables, chairs, bed and so on to sell in the market. That means surely Jesus was not involved in something which is inherently corrupt.

Then, why should God create a business? God created a business so that we could reflect God's love through our business. We could accomplish God's purpose through our business. In the early days, people used to practice barter system (exchange goods for goods). That was the way of meeting one another's need. But, through the times it has changed and now, business is all about making profit as much as one can make. It has been abused due to human fallen nature. Businessmen gripe with greed. They are using all means such as globalization and various business policies to become richer and richer whereas poor are becoming poorer and poorer (Luke 12:16-21). Business has become a threat to human existence due to massive industries. We as Christians should not just talk about things, rather we should be taking action. There is a saying in India - "Iron Cuts Iron." In the same way, this problem which has been caused by industries can be solved by industries only, which will honor God. Money is power; and if this power goes into wrong hands, it can become a threat to whole humanity. This is actually happening right now. Being a Christian we should do business not just to provide for our family but to provide for those who are 'poor' (poor people are those, who cannot work, who are disabled, orphan, widow women, old people, and those who are not aware or not able to use the local resources that are available to them) among us (Ephesians 4:28). We should do business for a good cause, which will bring glory and honor to God.

There can be three aspects of poverty: *spiritual poverty, physical poverty,* and *ecological poverty or surrounding neighborhood poverty.* Poverty is the by-product of the fall. It is the consequence of disobedience, and more importantly an impression of God's judgment. Christians should do business for the kingdom of God, which is moving towards the new heaven and a new earth, rather than self-seeking and self-centered business. We see one of the characteristics of social entrepreneurs is that they do not store or earn wealth for themselves (Matthew 6:19-21). Social Entrepreneurship follows as the best biblical business model, to make this earth a better place to live in, since its motive is to bring liberation and restoration in our community and to the creation.

4.5. Social Entrepreneurship as Missional

During the breakdown of the Roman Empire, the Christian philosopher Augustine (354-430) wrote a piece of writing titled *The City of God* in which he described two "cities". On one hand, there is an *earthly city*, which represents a way of life that is driven by self-love and contempt for God. People of the earthly city are unhappy and experience despair since earthly notions of self-love are so distorted and misguided. On the other, there is a *heavenly city* which is a way of life that glorifies God and is ultimately achieved in the afterlife. While on earth, followers of the heavenly city live a God-centered life and work to advance towards God's kingdom. This defines who they are, and gives a meaning to their lives that followers of the earthly city cannot experience.

Firstly, these are typically group-efforts among a community of believers, rather than being simply isolated campaigns of individual people. It is often this connection with a larger group that gives believers a sense of belonging that they would not otherwise have, and thus enhances their sense of life's meaning.

Secondly, there is devotion to a firm and sacred set of beliefs about God's role in human affairs. While theories about the nature and existence of God are many, not just any view of God will do. Leaders within these religious traditions formulate precise doctrines, and believers pledge exclusive devotion to them, thereby rejecting the views of rival religious groups. By embracing these sacred doctrines, believers see themselves as embarking on a higher mission from God and not just participating in routine human-created social activity.

Thirdly, participating in this higher mission involves self-sacrifice. Furthering God's kingdom is no easy task: it is financially costly, time consuming, and mission efforts are commonly met with brutal opposition. Yet, by enduring these hardships, believers feel a special accomplishment when they make progress.

While the notion of "furthering God's kingdom" is distinctly religious in nature, there are many non-religious groups that similarly try to transform society through some moral or political ideology. Like religious missions, these involve group efforts among like-minded people who are devoted to a precise higher calling and willingly endure hardship. Some of these social causes are preserving the environment, eliminating poverty, defending political freedoms, ending minority oppression, or creating global harmony. Devotees of these ideologies often gain a sense of life's meaning similar to that of their religious counterparts, but they do not have solid foundations for the things that they are doing. Whereas Christians have a foundation in their work for the sake of the gospel.

We know social entrepreneurs have a purpose beyond profit, and that could certainly come from spiritual beliefs. Social entrepreneurs move with empathy since their whole intention for creating a venture is to redeem those people who are neglected by our society or by the government, restore them, and make them sustainable out of love just as God's creation is an expression of His love.

Christian Social Entrepreneurships are one of the best practices to reach-out to unreached people groups. Missionaries today are forming trades or occupations that will enable them to do missions work. This isn't simply for the sake of financial support; it is also to keep the government from expelling them from the country for illegal conduct such as proselytizing, distributing illegal literature, and being missionaries. The old model of "business as missions" is not at all social entrepreneurship; it is merely a means of getting in, where as social entrepreneurship is a means of ministering to the people of that country. The old model (Business as Mission) was a door *to* ministry while the new model (Christian Social Entrepreneurship) *is* ministry since its nature is Missional.

4.6. Examples or Few Models of Social Entrepreneurship

There are many Social Entrepreneurs working around the world. Following are some of the existing models.

1. LifeBread

"Give a man a fish," the saying goes, "and you will feed him for a day. Teach a man how to fish and you will feed him for a lifetime." *Dusty Breeding* founder of LifeBread followed this principle. Breeding first visited Africa in 2006, working with orphans and other malnourished children. He was so moved by the heartbreaking conditions he experienced that he decided to use his culinary arts background to help the children learn to bake bread for their own nourishment and to help lift themselves out of poverty. The nonprofit organization Breeding founded, LifeBread Inc., is dedicated to empowering the people of impoverished nations through nutritional education and food preparation training as a means to curb the severity of world hunger. Breeding is enthusiastic about the use of solar ovens in his programs to promote a better ecosystem, and hopes to eventually equip an orphanage with a large commercial model capable of baking 400 loaves of bread daily.

Life Bread combines social entrepreneurship with missionary work. This kind of social entrepreneurship combines relief work, constructive community building, and sustainable solutions. "We feed people because we love God," he said. Breeding modeled LifeBread after the actions of Jesus throughout the Gospels. He said because Jesus met the physical and spiritual needs of the masses out of his love for God, he also decided to persure his personal calling to serve. Breeding said, his crew and him, serve those in need out of love for their faith and a passion for Christ's message. Once the ovens and bakeries are built, the LifeBread team gives classes in culinary work and sustainability, paired with Bible classes to foster spiritual development. LifeBread is a highly developed missionary work. The team builds and teaches but additionally instills a lasting imprint of Christ's love and community sustainability. With two running bakeries in Western Uganda and Nairobi in Kenya, Breeding and the LifeBread team continue to reach further and dream bigger.

2. The Loft Coffee House

The Loft Coffee House just outside San Antonio serves fresh pastries, a full lunch, a waffle bar, coffee and specialty drinks on Saturday mornings. Most people are unaware at first that this enterprise is actually a work of Riverside, a United Methodist Church. In fact, Riverside was birthed out of The Loft Coffee House. The Loft Coffee House stated a goal to "provide a quiet respite, a place for community gatherings and activities to give back locally and internationally, to breathe life into others" (Gosnell 2010). The Loft wanted to engage the culture and create community instead of following the older church model of erecting a church building and assuming people would come. The Loft has drawn people who would not normally be drawn to a church. They have also provided a space for Bible studies, mom's groups, and teenage groups. They not only began a church, but they formed the Hope Center—a combination thrift store, food pantry, and social service resource referral service. They are meeting social, economic, and spiritual needs.

3. Christian HELP

Christian HELP is a Central Florida non-profit organization, started by a couple who felt called to minister outside of the church. The founders were local entrepreneurs who were at crossroads, deciding if they wanted to continue in business or not. They really felt God tugging at them to minister outside of the church and after speaking with their pastor, they decided to minister the unemployed by providing for their material and spiritual needs. This ministry has continued to grow in terms of helping people find jobs, strengthening their job skills, tweaking their resumes, as well as developing their faith.

4. Alberto Cairo: International Committee of the Red Cross, Orthopedic Center

Alberto Cario was growing up in Northern Italy. His mother encouraged him to help those who are less fortunate than him. He took this advice to heart and by chance became intrigued with physical therapy. He initially wanted to become a lawyer but he was more attracted towards and felt more satisfied on becoming a physical therapist. So, he quits his law practice and got a degree in physical therapy and went to Sudan to work with the children who were of war. He was kicked out by Sudanese government but later he joined ICRC and went to Afghanistan. When he reached there, he wanted to work among the landmine victims there, but soon he realized, he was there for a big purpose.

He stopped crying when patients came in with missing limbs or old wounds that have been left untreated for months or even years. He found carrying on depleted the energy that he needed to help them get back on their feet. When someone crawls in there on his hands and knees with little hope for the future, he knows that with their help, victims can walk out of that place with prosthesis and there are possibilities of a meaningful life. While his life there was very hard, "it is in giving of myself, that I receive so much more joy and satisfaction in return," says Cairo.

The center thought, as a member of the same human race, they must treat each patient's social and physical needs as a whole. All of their staff personnel are disabled. Imagine how much better you would feel when you realize that the staff member greets you at the center has only one arm, the physical therapist who asks about your future, his legs are missing, and each of them giving you big smile. They encourage disabled children to go to school. For those above school age, they provide vocational training. Their home-care program for those who cannot take care of themselves provides medical, economic, social and psychological rehabilitation. They also have a program for children with cerebral palsy. Cairo's infectious laugh and gentle touch make him a favorite among his patients.

However, over the years, he has come to realize that, when you lose a limb, a bit of your life, your heart, and your mind are also lost. And while you can be given a plastic leg easily enough, who is going to give you back the other things? Most of the amputees we see are men between the ages of 20 and 35: the years when they marry, become fathers, and are working to support themselves and their dependents. All of a sudden they lose everything, perhaps forever. They are dependent on others, the future looks bleak. In Afghanistan, there are no insurance schemes, no health service, and no social assistance. Are these not valid causes for despair? Many disabled people recover from depression when given a job or a micro-loan to start a business. Others fail to respond to our attempts. Thanks to the dedication of the Afghan workers, who are almost all ex-patients and themselves disabled.

Since 1997, they had offered microcredit loans of up to Rs. 48,800 to their patients to help them start their own businesses. The ICRT was at first reluctant to provide funds for microloans so Cairo asked if he could use the money due to him for vacation days he had not taken. They permitted this and are now pleased with the results and have decided that they will now provide all the funds. Their loans are interest-free to the recipients. They started by providing loans to quadriplegics who seldom ventured outside. They provide them with small trolleys and a few goods to sell and it was a great success. They have a 95% repayment rate. Some of their disabled staff bicycle as much as sixty kilometers in a day checking on the progress of our microloan recipients. They now have jobs and also dignity and empathy for those they now serve, making and fitting artificial limbs for over 2,000 other disabled people who come to the ICRC center each year. They also help reintegrate patients into society by providing job training and micro-credit loans.

They have no problems with the different political regimes that have controlled Afghanistan over the past thirty years because they know that they are doing something good for the people and have no political agenda. Everyone is welcome here. Cairo recalls one man who came to the center with injuries caused while fighting the Russians. He later returned dressed as Taliban and more recently came to them dressed in western clothes.

Alberto Cairo is a social entrepreneur. His work definitely reflects the heart of God towards these war victims. He is not only treating them but also giving them a hope to live, smiles, laugh and dream. He has not only helped them stand on their own feet but given them a tool to self-sustain and live their life with dignity and respect with greater hope.

5. Sari Bari

Sari Bari is a business offering freedom to women who are working in the sex trade and to young women who are vulnerable to trafficking. The business provides a safe loving environment where women are trained as artisans. The women create beautiful, sustainable, handmade products while renewing their lives. Each Sari Bari product, whether it be a blanket, accessory, or baby item, is sewn using the traditional "Kantha stitch." All its products are unique—there are no two pieces exactly alike. Each piece is an investment of time, skill, creativity, and patience. Each woman stitches her nametag onto the finished product, marking its completion as a work of art and the pride with which she sends it out for each Sari Bari customer to enjoy.

Sari Bari was opened in 2006, in Kolkata, India by Co-founders Sarah Lance and Kristin Keen. Sari Bari was created in response to the dire need for alternatives to women desiring to exit the sex trade. Kolkata hosts more than 22 red light areas and more than 60,000 women work in its commercial sex industry. Sari Bari was born out of meeting girls like Pinkie, a young girl encountered in the red light area. She was so young, looking raw and humiliated, with tears welling in her eyes. Poverty had led her to the sex trade to support her sick father and two brothers. Our hearts broke, and we were moved to action. The names and stories like that of Pinkie's have become the foundation of Sari Bari's work for their freedom.

Sari Bari provides a safe haven for survivors, allowing them learn a new trade and get an education. Sari Bari started with three women, now employs more than 100 women, and is still growing. The business is comprised of four manufacturing units: three in red light areas and one in a rural source trafficking area. It hopes to continue growing in the area of prevention, having opened another Prevention Manufacturing Unit in 2015.

Their mission is to empower economically vulnerable women through artisan enterprises by bringing handmade creative, beautiful, proud and passionate artisans who have overcome the perils of abuse, conflict, and disease. By assisting local partners around the world in bringing these goods "to the market," they take an active role in equipping the survivors they employ with economic independence while raising awareness of the challenges that they face.

Their model is, Promoting survivor-made goods "TO THE MARKET" via multiple distribution channels, including pop-up shops, custom sourcing, retail partnerships, and our online marketplace; Their main aim is offer a platform for survivors and their champions to share their stories with a new, larger audience reaching their eyes, ears, and hearts, through TTM's Stories and Huffington Post blogs, and providing tailored services to our Local Partners utilising trend forecasting and basic mental health resources to improve production and management.

Conclusion

According to Justin J. Evans, in "The Facts and Stats on 33,000 Denominations," more than 33,000 denominations in the world are dependent on charity. There is no doubt that Christians are doing a great deal of mission work. However, it becomes imperative that mission must be, without violating biblical principles; oriented or tuned according to the demanding situation of our time. It would be such a failure if all the above charity has a focus on self-promotion. This will be against the Kingdom standard.

Social entrepreneurship is very much oriented to mission in reflecting the heart of God. Mission agencies and missionaries can develop social entrepreneurship as an alternative model for an innovative and sustainable Christian mission work in areas such as health care, education, fair trade, human rights and social justice, disaster management and rehabilitation, environment and the restoration of a sustainable planet, among many others. The prospect of future mission must transcend mere charity and encompass social, economic and spiritual spheres. The risk the Christian Social Entrepreneur is willing to take is like the cross Jesus was willing to bear for the hope of change. Risk equates the dream being born and the hope for Kingdom causes and the Mission of God being accomplished in society. Christian Social Entrepreneurship is the way to bring redemption and restoration into the society for common good of all. It can be done in a sustainable way through creative ventures and by introducing faith and Kingdom principles to the society.

References

Baer, Michael R. *Business as Mission: The Power of Business in the Kingdom of God.* Seattle: YWAM Publishing, 2006.

Bankoti, T. S. *Chipko Movement.* New Delhi: GVPH, 2008.

Bansal, Rashmi. *Connect the Dots: Inspiring Stories of 20 Entrepreneurs without an MBA who Dared to Find their Own Path.* Chennai: Westland, 2012.

______________. *Follow Every Rainbow: The inspiring stories of 25 women entrepreneurs whose gentle touch created strong business.* Chennai: Westland, 2013.

______________. *I have a Dream: The Inspiring Stories of 20 Social Entrepreneurs who found New Ways to Solve the Old Problems.* Chennai: Westland, 2011.

______________. *Stay Hungry Stay Foolish: The Inspiring Stories of 25 IIM Ahmedabad graduates who choose to tread path of their own making.* Chennai: Westland, 2012.

________________. *Take Me Home: The Inspiring Stories of 20 Entrepreneurs from Small-Town India With Big-Time Dreams.* Chennai: Westland, 2014.

Ben Witherington III, *Jesus and Money: A Guide for Times of Financial* Crises. Grand Rapids, Michigan: Brazos Press, 2010.

Benioff, Marc and Southwick, Karen. *Compassionate Capitalism: How Corporations Can Make Doing Good an Integral Part of Doing Well.* New Jersey: Career Press, 2004.

Benjamin, Paul Solomon S. *Business as Mission: Resource Mobilization for Sustainability.* Delhi: ISPCK, 2015.

Bhargave, Shivganesh, ed. *Developmental Aspects of Entrepreneurship.* New Delhi: Sage Publication, 2007.

Blackaby, Henry T. Willis, Avery T. Blackaby, Jr. *On Mission with God.* Nashville: Broadman and Holman Publisher, 2001.

Bornstein David and Davis Susan. *Social Entrepreneurship: What Everyone Needs to Know.* New York: Oxford Press, 2010.

Bornstein, David. *How to Change the World: Social Entrepreneurs and the Power of New Ideas.* New York: Oxford University Press, 2007.

Burns, Paul. *Corporate Entrepreneurship: Innovation and Strategy in Large Organization.* Haryana: Replika Press, 2013.

C. K. Prahalad. *The Fortune at the Bottom of the Pyramid: Eradicating Poverty through Profits.* Delhi: Dorling Kindersley, 2006.

Danielson, Robert A. *The Social Entrepreneur: The Business of Changing the World.* Tennesse: Seedbed Publishing, 2015.

Danielson, Robert A., ed. *The Social Entrepreneur: The Business of Changing the world.* Kentucky: Seed Bed Publishing, 2015.

Dees, Gregory J., Jed Emerson and Peter Economy. *Enterprising Nonprofits: A Toolkit for Social Entrepreneurs.* New York: John Wiley & Sons, 2002.

Duzer Van, Jeff. *Why Business Matters to God: And What Still Needs to Be Fixed.* Illinois: InterVersity Press, 2010.

Fayolle, Alain, and Harry Matlay. Eds. *Handbook of Research on Social Entrepreneurship.* Massachusetts: Edward Elgar Publishing, Inc., 2010.

Follett, Mary Parker, ed. *On Social Entrepreneurship: Center for Business Ethics at Bentley College.* Malden: Blackwell Publishing, 2009.

Gilpin, Robert. *Global Political Economy.* New Jersey: Princeton University Press, 2001.

Gonzalez, Justo L. *Faith and Wealth.* New York: Harper Collins Publishers, 1990.

Grudem, Wayne. *Business for the Glory of God.* Wheaton, Illinois: Crossway books, 2003.

Hedlund, Roger E. *Roots of the Great Debate in Mission: Mission in Historical and Theological Perspective.* Bangalore: Theological Book Trust, 1993.

Horsley, Richard A. *Covenant Economics: A Biblical Vision of Justice for all.* Kenttucky: WJK, 2009.

Jamir, Menjiwapong. *Understanding the Jesus Movement in the Gospel Tradition.* Kolkata: ESPACE, 2013.

Johnson, Kevin D. *The Entrepreneur Mind: 100 Essential Beliefs, Characteristics and habits of Elite Entrepreneurs.* Mehta Road, Mumbai: Jaico Publishing house, 2013.

Longkumer, Limatula, ed. *Good News to the Whole Creation.* New Delhi: ISPCK, 2016.

Mair, Johanna and Jeffrey Robinson, eds.," *Social Entrepreneurship.* New York: Palgrave Macmillan, 2006.

Mancur, Olson. *The Logic of Collective Action.* Cambridge: Harvard University Press, 1965.

Mtata, Kenneth. *Dignity of Work: Theological and Interdisciplinary Perspectives.* Minnesota: Lutheran University Press, 2011.

Nicholls, Alex, ed. *Social Entrepreneurship New Models of Sustainable Social Change.* New York: Oxford University Press Inc., 2006.

Peters, George W. *A Biblical Theology of Missions.* Chicago: Moody Publishers, 1972.

Peverelli, Peter. J. and Song, Jiwen. *Chinese Entrepreneurship: A Social Capital Approach*. Verlag Berlin Heidelberg: Springer, 2012.

Prahalad, C. K. *The Fortune at the Bottom of the Pyramid: Eradicating Poverty through Profits*. Delhi: Dorling Kindersley, 2006.

Praszkier, Ryszard, and Andrzej Nowak. *Social Entrepreneurship: Theory and Practice*. New York: Cambridge University Press, 2012.

Reinders, Adrie, and Freijsen Marion. *The E. Factor: Entrepreneurship in Social Media Age*. Dallas, TX: Ben Bella, 2012.

Renick, M. S. *Christian Missionary Movement in Northern India*. Delhi: ISPCK, 2004.

Robert, Gilpin. *Global Political Economy*. New Jersey: Princeton University Press, 2001.

Sahu, Dhirendra Kumar. *Christian Faith and Economic Justice*. Mumbai: Bombay Urban Industrial League for Development, 1996.

Schaeffer, Francis A. *Genesis in Space & Time*. Illinois: InterVarsity Press, 1972.

Swarr, Bentch Sharon and Nordstorm Dwight. *Transform the World: Biblical Vision and Purpose for Business*. Richmond, VA: The Center for Entrepreneurship and Economic Development, 1999.

Tennent, Timothy C. *Invitation to World Mission: A Trinitarian Missiology for the Twenty-first Century*. Grand Rapids, MI: Kregel Publications, 2010.

Volkmann, C.K. ed., *Social Entrepreneurship and Social Business*. Gabler Verlag: Springer Fachmedien Wiesbaden, 2012.

Webber, Robert E. *The Church in the World: Opposition, Tension or Transformation?* Michigan: Academic Books, 1986.

Witherington, Ben III. *Jesus and Money: A Guide for Times of Financial* Crises. Grand Rapids, Michigan: Brazos Press, 2010.

Yunus, Muhammad. *Creating a World without Poverty: Social Business and the Future of capitalism*. New York: Public Affairs, 2007.

Internet

"Mission Focus: Social Entrepreneurship." *Bethany Global University*, https://bethanygu.edu/news/missions-focus-social-entrepreneurship/, accessed on 3 January 2016.

"Social Enterprise," *Mission Australia: Together We Stand*, https://www.missionaustralia.com.au/what-we-do/employment-skills-training/social-enterprise, accessed on 2 December 2016.

"Social Entrepreneurship from Christian Prospective," http://www.gtfeducation.org/images/dynamic/file/Social-Enterprise-Electronic-Monograph1.pdf?1325905656887, accessed on 4 December, 2016.

"To the Market: Survivor-Made Goods." http://www.tothemarket.com/our-journey/about accessed 26 November 2016.

"Turning A Business Trend into Transformed Lives." *Denver Institute for Faith and work,* http://denverinstitute.org/2015/07/13/social-entrepreneurship-turning-a-business-trend-into-transformed-lives/, accessed on 4 December 2016.

Bavisotto, Mark. "Was Jesus the Greatest Social Entrepreneur of All Time." https://www.linkedin.com/pulse/jesus-greatest-social-entrepreneur-all-time-mark-bavisotto, accessed 7 October 2016.

Blanchard Dave and Kwan, Josh. "The Washington Post," https://www.washingtonpost.com/local/praxis-fellows-inspired-by-christian-faith-build-organizations-for-socialchange/2012/04/11/gIQARSrXAT_story.html?utm_term=.48a0ab8930dd, accessed on 5 December 2016.

Business as Mission. "7 *Markers for a Kingdom Business: A Framework for Entrepreneurs,*" http://businessasmission.com/7-markers-kingdom-business/, accessed on 4 December 2016.

Christian Help. "Finding Job, Reducing Hunger, Providing Hope," http://www.christianhelp.org/, accessed on 5 December 2016.

Christian Theological Seminary, "Social Entrepreneurship for Mission and not for Profit work", https://www.eventbrite.com/e/social-entrepreneurship-for-mission-and-not-for-profit-work-tickets-25838908872, accessed on 3 December 2016.

Evans, Justin J. "The Facts and Stats on 33,000 Denominations." http://www.philvaz.com/apologetics/a106.htm, accessed on 25 November, 2016.

Fakhrul Anwar Zainol, et al., "Overcoming Poverty through Social Entrepreneurship: A Conceptual Paper," *International Business Research* 7/7; (2014), 183-188. http://dx.doi.org/10.5539/ibr.v7n7p183, accessed on 28 July 2016.

Fieser, James. "The Meaning of Life." https://www.utm.edu/staff/jfieser/class/120/1-meaning.htm, accessed on 5 December 2016.

JOYAN, http://www.joynindia.com/pages/about-us-test, accessed on Jan 2nd, 2017.

Keller, Tim. "God as an Entrepreneur: Humans Should Create as God Does." *Faith and Leadership: Theological Reflection* (May 31, 2010), https://www.faithandleadership.com/goods-and-god?page=full, accessed 10 October 2016.

Knowles, Susan J. "Jesus: A Social Entrepreneur," http://www.crosswalk.com/family/career/jesus-a-social-entrepreneur.html, accessed 7 October 2016.

Neubert, Mitchell J. "Entrepreneurs Feel Closer to God than the Rest of Us Do." https://hbr.org/2013/10/entrepreneurs-feel-closer-to-god-than-the-rest-of-us-do, accessed on 27 November, 2016.

Pacific Continental, "Social Enterprise: An Alternative Funding Strategy," https://www.therightbank.com/sites/www.therightbank.com/files/files/Business%20Resources/White%20Papers/Nonprofit/white-paper-social-enterprise-an-alternative-funding-strategy.pdf, accessed 12 august 2016.

Padilla, Rene C. "Holistic Mission: Occasional." In *Lausanne Committee for World Evangelization: The whole Church Taking the Whole Gospel to the Whole World,* paper no. 33, edited by Evvy Hay Campbell. Pattaya: Lausanne Committee for

World Evangelization, 2004), 15-16. https://www.lausanne.org/wp-content/uploads/2007/06/LOP33_IG4.pdf, Accessed on 31 October 2016.

Pepperdine Graphic. "Life Bread's social entrepreneurs follow in Christ's teachings," http://pepperdine-graphic.com/lifebreads-social-entrepreneurs-follow-in-christs teachings/, accessed on 5 December 2016.

Prahalad, C. K. "Michigan to Expand World View," *Dividend* 38 (Fall 2013): 38. https://deepblue.lib.umich.edu/bitstream/handle/2027.42/50785/2003-fall-dividend.pdf?sequence=1&isAllowed=y, accessed on 18 September, 2016.

Quizlet, "World Cultures 9/10 H1.3," https://quizlet.com/93067254/world-cultures-910-h-13-flash-cards/, accessed on 12 December 2016.

Rebecca Rigal, McQuigg. "Why Social Entrepreneurs Could Use a Little More Faith," https://www.good.is/articles/why-social-entrepreneurs-could-use-a-little-more-faith, accessed 10 October 2016.

Rigal, McQuigg, Rebecca. "Why Social Entrepreneurs Could Use a Little More Faith." https://www.good.is/articles/why-social-entrepreneurs-could-use-a-little-more-faith, accessed on 10 October 2016.

Sari Bari. "To the market: Survivor-Made goods," http://www.tothemarket.com/saribari (accessed 26 November, 2016).

Sari Bari. "To the market: Survivor-Made goods," http://www.tothemarket.com/saribari, accessed on 26 November 2016.

Smile, Thomas. "10 Traits All Successful Entrepreneurs Share." https://www.entrepreneur.com/article/243792, accesses 5 august 2016.

Social Earth, "Company List", http://socialearth.org/company-list, accessed on 5 December 2016.

Susan J. Knowles. "Jesus: A Social Entrepreneur." http://www.crosswalk.com/family/career/jesus-a-social-entrepreneur.html, accessed 7 October 2016.

Thompson, "Julia Value & Capitalism." http://www.valuesandcapitalism.com/the-secret-to-success-for-social-entrepreneurs-innovative-obedience/, accessed on 5 December 2016.

Zainol, Anwar Fakhrul et al. Editors. "Overcoming Poverty through Social Entrepreneurship: A Conceptual Paper." *International Business Research* 7/7 (2014). http://dx.doi.org/10.5539/ibr.v7n7p183 accessed on 28 July -2016.

Zoominfo. "Dusty Breeding," http://www.zoominfo.com/p/Dusty-Breeding/1357913424, accessed on 5 December 2016.